Introduction to the Adult

Overview

FILLING IN THE BLANKS... A Guided Look at Growing Up Adopted is a special book. After five years of research, writing, and revising, it's finally ready! Here is a tool that we believe will be of value to families formed by any variety of adoption. It is appropriate for children adopted as infants and those adopted at an older age; for parent couples and single adoptors; for those whose adoptions were facilitated by agencies or those which were independent; for domestic or international adoptions running the spectrum from traditional and closed to the most innovative and open. Be prepared to be patient in using it. This is not a project to be completed in a day or two, a weekend, or several days. This is a project to be worked on in manageable segments over weeks, months— in some cases even years!

The very nature of the book makes it necessary for you to prepare to use it. You are probably a parent, social worker, counselor, therapist, or teacher. You may have lots of experience with lifebooks and with adoption stories. You may have little or no experience with these things. Whatever the case, please carefully read this introduction. **Before you begin working on the book with the child, be sure to tear out these introductory pages. They are for you only and should not be left in the child's book.**

This book is primarily intended for children aged 10-14 who were adopted. However, it should be recognized that children, their needs, interests and abilities vary greatly. Some nine year olds with good reading abilities and maturity levels may benefit from the book. Some fourteen year olds with poor reading abilities and maturity levels may not be ready for the book. In the end, you as the adult will have to decide if the child is ready to understand the information presented in the book as well as to deal with the emotions that may arise while completing this book.

Be sensitive to the needs and abilities of the child. If you get started and find the child frustrated and not wanting to sit and work on the book, then that might be a sign that the child may not be ready for it. It might also be a sign that the child is uncomfortable with some of the issues in this book. Should this happen, you might consider consulting others (a social worker, teacher, another family, or a therapist) to find out if the child's frustration is due to lack of maturity, reading and writing

problems, emotional difficulty with the topic, or a combination of difficulties.

If the child is, indeed, not ready for this project, feel free to put it aside for a while. In doing so, you will be doing the child a favor. You will be recognizing his lack of readiness and you will be protecting him from frustration. This need to put the book aside may come at different times for different children. For some, you may decide to put it aside immediately after reading this introduction. For other children, the need could arise at any time during the project. Some children may be able to complete the entire book without long breaks. Use this introductory material to help you determine when it is wise to give the child a break from working on the book.

FILLING IN THE BLANKS should never be given to a child to complete alone. Children need help to find the information the book requires, to deal with the emotions some of the sections may bring forth, and to choose the most appropriate pages at the most appropriate times. You should *always* work on the book with the child. In doing so, it's helpful to carefully follow the guidelines in this introduction. This introductory material will help you with the following things:

1. the structure of the book
2. the preferred methods for use
3. who should use the book with the child
4. common questions about the book (and their answers)
5. using the book with the children with special needs
6. planning your use of the book

Structure of the Book

There are four major sections in *FILLING IN THE BLANKS*. Each section contains smaller sub-sections that are each usually no more than one or two pages long. These sub-sections are marked with numbers inside an illustration of a sunrise:

The first section, MY BIRTH FAMILY, deals with the child's family of birth and adoption issues related to that. Knowing as much as possible about birth families can help give children and their families a better understanding of each other. This book will help you

1

to know what information to obtain. The social worker who helped with your adoption is a good source for knowing where and if you can actually obtain birth family information. Local parent support groups can also be helpful here.

The second section is MY ADOPTION PROCESS. It tells about various types of adoption, how different types of adoptions happen, and how the child's own adoption happened. This section can be an enjoyable one for parent and child to do together.

The third section is MY ADOPTIVE FAMILY. It contains information about the child's adoptive family, such as family traditions, family members, family values and commitment, and family time. Again, this section can be fun to do.

The final section is MY SELF. This section can help the child understand what it means to be an individual. It deals with issues such as self-esteem, being unique, growing and changing in several ways, peer pressure.

Within each section is a unique structure that needs explanation. As you read a section, you will find that it contains smaller sub-sections each of which can be used singly or with all other sub-sections. For example, the BIRTH FAMILY section contains six sub-sections. Some are, "Questions About Birth Parents," "Birth Brothers and Sisters," and "Why Adoption?" Each sub-section is about the right length for finishing in one sitting. This will be true for children who are 10-14 years old. If the child is younger, a shorter sitting may be required. If the child has difficulty with reading or writing or with the adoption issues, you may need to spend less time at work. You can be sensitive to the child's needs while deciding how long to work on the book.

Important words are identified in each section of the book, so a thorough understanding of the use of those words is important. Each section begins with an introduction. Each sub-section begins with word definitions. (You will find a complete glossary of words and definitions at the end of the book. Do read through it before beginning to use the book with a child.) The child is instructed to discuss the words and definitions with the adult who is helping. Each word is defined clearly and positively so as to give new meanings to adoption terms that may at one time have had negative connotations.

For example, "birth parents" were once thought of as "natural parents" or "real parents". This terminology has been confusing. Adoptive parents can be just as "natural" or "real". So, the definition of "birth parents" in this book is, "The mother and father who give life to a baby. Everyone has a birth mother and birth father. Some people are nurtured by their birth parents. Other people are nurtured by their adoptive parents." (The word nurtured is also defined in light of adoption and its meanings.) This tells the child that although we all have birth parents, we are not all nurtured by those two people.

The way we talk about adoption, the words we choose to use, and the meanings we give to those words can be important in forming positive opinions and images about adoption. Hopefully, this way of dealing with the language of adoption will form a set of positive concepts and definitions within the child's mind. It is also hoped that adults using FILLING IN THE BLANKS will become more aware of the positive ways to talk and think about adoption.

Determining Methods for Use

There are many, many ways this book can be used. Even the thorough explanations here are probably incomplete. Yet, different possibilities need to be explored. It's important when deciding how to use the book that you remember to be flexible. You may choose one method of use, begin it, and find the child unable to continue. At that point, determine which other method would be best and try it. If you or the child feel frustrated, you may want to think of consulting another parent or a professional for some advice and support. Flexibility with and sensitivity to the child are most important while using FILLING IN THE BLANKS. The book is designed for use in any of the following ways, or any combination of the following.

1. Sequential Use

For this style of use, the book is worked through in order. This may be best for the child with no major adoption-related problems who feels comfortable learning about and discussing issues like birth parents. Parents, too, need to be ready to explore all aspects of FILLING IN THE BLANKS to be able to move sequentially through the book. For this method of use, child and parent must feel secure and safe learning about things to which there may be no sure answers.

Another reason this may be the best way to use the book is that the ideas in the book build upon one another. As each new sub-section unfolds, new adoption issues are discussed. If a child enters the book in the middle, it can be more difficult to follow some ideas, because they may have been introduced in an earlier section. This will be especially true of the ADOPTION PROCESS and ADOPTIVE FAMILY sections.

Sequential use is the easiest way to use the book and the easiest situation in which to use it, but many families will not be able to use the book this way. If you wonder whether you can, ask someone whose advice you can trust.

2. Need-Oriented Use

For this type of use, the adult working with the child determines the child's current needs in order of priority. Then the adult finds the sections of the book that will meet those needs. Many children will need this method, including those with problem adoptions, children with birth parent difficulties, pre-adolescents who are increasingly insecure.

Here, upon deciding where the child needs to begin, you merely go to that section of the book and begin, sub-section by sub-section, until you have completed the whole section. Then, review the needs of the child and go to the next appropriate section. Thus, a child who expresses a deep need to know as much as possible about the new family would possibly want to begin in the ADOPTIVE FAMILY section. A child with fears and concerns about birth family might be in need of the BIRTH FAMILY section first. Working through the difficult emotions about birth parents, their existence, reasons for choosing adoption, and how the child feels would all be helpful.

When using this method, be sure to work from the first sub-section through to the last. Information within each sub-section builds in order. Ideas that are presented in the beginning of the section will develop as the section moves along. The child may not be able to get the most out of the book unless sections are completed as wholes.

Need-oriented use of FILLING IN THE BLANKS is probably one of the best options for many children. Parents should remember that they should feel free to talk with a trusted friend or professional who understands adoption if there are questions or concerns as they continue to work with their child.

3. Child-Determined Use

Many adults may shy away from letting a child decide which sections will be done and when. However, this can be a good option. A good time to use this method is when a child is feeling a loss of control. So often children, especially those adopted at an older age, feel somewhat helpless. They often feel they are moved, adopted, and counseled at the whim of the adults in control. That can be frightening. Giving control where possible can help.

To let the child determine which sections to do and in what order, the adult would first look over the entire book with the child. Each section would be explored together so that the child could make a well-informed decision. Then, the decision would be made. An agreement about which sections would be done and in what order would be made. Thus, the topics the child are reluctant to discuss (which will probably be at the end of the list) would still be included, and the child and you would know that they will be discussed at some point. The discussion may come later than you wish, but it will come. Some children are quite capable of determining which sections they prefer to do first. The decision may have nothing to do with problems of acceptance or denial, but rather, personal preference.

Consider this method for children who are older or emotionally mature, those who are not experiencing many adopted-related problems, or those who need to gain a feeling of some control over their lives. (Note: Although a need to gain a sense of control could be adoption-related, for these purposes, please consider it a separate issue.)

4. Birth/Arrival to Adolescence Use

This may be the preferred method, especially for those who were adopted as young children. For this use, the parent acquires FILLING IN THE BLANKS at or before the adoption of the child, whether the adoption was in infancy or at a later date. At that time, the parent thoroughly reads the book to become familiar with the things that the child will be reading later. Then, the parent begins to use the language and concepts of the book every day.

For example, instead of waiting until the child asks about birth parents, the parent talks about it early on as though it was a fact of life like any other fact of life. And indeed it is! Some families talk about birth parents as soon as their children begin to understand about babies growing in their mother's bodies. When those talks begin (today they begin as early as two and three), adoptive parents can talk with the child about how the child's birth mother carried the child in her body.

By having and knowing FILLING IN THE BLANKS from the time of the adoption, parents can be better prepared to be honest and positive with their children and with themselves. (Having the book then also helps the parent to ask the right questions of adoption workers to gain information the child will later need to complete the book. Knowing what information to request helps workers to know what to find out.) Thus, from the time the adoption occurs until the age of eight or nine, the ideas, concepts, and language of FILLING IN THE BLANKS are the ideas, concepts, and language of the adoptive family.

The next step is to bring the book out at about the age of ten or so. At this point don't be in a hurry to finish the book. Take months or even years to complete it. Use one or several of the first three methods to complete FILLING IN THE BLANKS with the child. You might move in order through the book. If that isn't best, decide which sections the child would need the most. Or, let the child decide which section to do. Remember to complete sections in order for the best results. Savor the time spent together working on the book. Don't rush!

Determining Which Adult Should Help with the Book Use

Deciding who should complete this book with the child need not be difficult. There are many choices. Again, a combination of choices might be the best option. Here are some suggestions for how to determine which adult should work with the child.

1. Parent(s) and Child Alone

The choice of parent and child working together alone would be the best in families where parents have positive attitudes toward most aspects of the adoption. Parents might wish to consult with an adoption worker or other adoptive parents about certain questions they have while working on the book. New adoptive parents, too, can benefit from contact with an experienced adoptive parent. Concerns may arise while working on this book for which a parent experienced in adoption can provide support and advice.

Adoptive parent support groups often provide help for new adoptive families. One type of support could be to introduce FILLING IN THE BLANKS to the new family and to offer guidance. Or, the new adoptive family could turn to the support group if and when some advice is needed about how to deal with birth information and other concerns.

The parent support group could even be helpful in working with adoption workers to locate new adoptive parents, give them FILLING IN THE BLANKS or tell them about it, and offer support.

Some adoptive parents, after a very short time, seem to find many families who have adopted and who can be supportive in an informal way. Parents might wish to turn to those friends for advice.

2. Parent and Child with Helping Professional

Here, a parent realizes that there are some sub-sections in FILLING IN THE BLANKS that parent or child will find uncomfortable. This realization may come before beginning work on the book. It may also come after work has already begun. For these uncomfortable times, a helping professional could be of assistance. Problem sub-sections could be identified by carefully looking at the parent's and child's concerns. Then, the helping professional could complete these with the child. Helping professionals to turn to for this might be social workers, family therapists, and teachers (in the case of children with reading and writing difficulties.)

In many cases, professional support can be used less and less as the family becomes more comfortable. Sometimes it can be difficult to accept help from a professional. Families should not, however, be reluctant to ask for help when it is needed.

3. Child with Helping Professional

A few parents and children will find it difficult to complete this book together. This can be because of parental concerns or the child's own difficulties. In this case a helping professional like a social worker or therapist may be able to help the child, at least through the parts which are most difficult for him. Some children who were adopted find it very difficult to discuss the issue of their birth family. Others may have difficulty with the topics of the adoption process or new family. Some children have difficulty sharing personal problems. Whatever the reason, these children may benefit from help by a professional who understands adoption and its issues. As always, professionals need to involve parents in this process and in the decisions that are made. In some situations, counseling for the child and/or family may eventually help the family to work on the book together.

4. Parent and Child with Teacher

It is possible that some teachers may have good reason to work on FILLING IN THE BLANKS with their students who were adopted. If so, the teacher should obtain permission to do so from the parents and should stay in close contact with the parents and include them in the process. When dealing with sensitive issues, close contact between home and school is a must. The teacher may also need assistance from helping professionals familiar with adoption and its issues.

Adoption workers (especially the child's adoption worker) and school social workers can be sources for help. It is unlikely, though, that a teacher will find the need to use *FILLING IN THE BLANKS* with most students.

A teacher will not usually be the one initiating the use of *FILLING IN THE BLANKS*. Rather, a family might find that a teacher may be able to be of assistance. Children with special needs, who are reluctant to read, or who have disabilities that affect reading and writing may need the assistance of a teacher. A teacher who understands the child's reading and writing difficulties can be helpful in completing this book.

Meeting Special Needs

Most parents and professionals who have children with special needs will know that these must be considered while planning a project like this book. if you are not sure whether the child has special needs, you might consider showing the child's teacher this book and asking for advice about the child's ability to work on it.

When a child does have special needs and you feel the need for some assistance, you could contact the child's special education teacher and discuss the project and enlist assistance in planning it. If you do not know who to contact, you could contact your local public school special education administration office for information. You might need to first call the general administrative offices of your school district or county to find out how to reach the special education offices. Other parents with children who have similar disabilities can be of help, too. Agencies or groups that could help include the local Association for Retarded Citizens, the local Association for Children and Adults with Learning Disabilities, and any local universities or colleges that have special education departments. If you want to locate another group that offers support for other special needs, your public school or local university or college could probably direct you. There are also many national networks for families with members who have disabilities that you could locate for information. Most libraries would have this information. These networks are usually listed by using the name of the disability with which they are concerned. This makes them easier to locate.

Children with special needs are each unique. Their needs are highly individual. Although some safe, general statements could be made about them, these state-ments (to be accurate) would be so general that there would be no specific helpful information for you. Whole textbooks have been written on the subjects of reading and writing with children in each disability category. Therefore, if you feel the need for help, quickly ask it of someone who can guide you and who can be available to answer questions as they arise during the course of the project.

As you search for assistance, there are some questions you will need to be able to ask. Remember that this is only a partial list of questions that will help you get the information you need.

1. Does my child have a disability that effects his reading and writing? What is it? What does it mean? Exactly how does it effect my child's reading and writing?

2. At what grade level does my child read? (This book is appropriate for children with reading abilities and maturity in the 10-14 age range.)

3. If my child reads at a lower level, what can I do to make the book comfortable reading? Should I read it to my child? Should I have the teacher help?

4. Can my child copy sentences? Compose and write sentences? If not, what can I do about the sections that require writing? Should I write as my child dictates? Should I let my child write a little and I help?

5. How long can my child pay attention to reading, writing, and thinking activities? (You could show the child's teacher some individual sub-sections of the book and ask for advice.)

6. Is my child developmentally ready for this book? If not, how can I adjust the maturity level of the book for my child? Or, should I wait a few months or years to begin work on the book? At what age might my child be ready for this book?

7. If your child has a visual impairment: Does my child need a large print or braille version of this book? If so, where can I obtain it?

8. If your child has a hearing impairment or is deaf: Does my child have the language growth necessary for using this book? If not, what can I do to make it usable?

9. If your child has a physical disability: How will my child's physical disability effect his or her ability to complete this book? Exactly how can I adjust the activities so that my child can use the book?

Tips for Using *FILLING IN THE BLANKS* with Children

Most parents and professionals have specific questions about *FILLING IN THE BLANKS.* Following you will find a list of common concerns and what you can do about them.

1. How long should each sitting be?

This is a very appropriate concern. Many adults are not sure how long children can sit and read and write. *FILLING IN THE BLANKS.* is even more demanding than a child's usual reading and writing. It requires a lot of serious thinking and emotional energy.

A simple guide to use is to plan to start with one sub-section at each sitting. Sub-sections in *FILLING IN THE BLANKS* have been designed to last about as long as 10 - 14 year olds usually have attention for school topics. If the child needs no extra help in school, receives positive reports from teachers about his ability to pay attention, to read, and to write, compared to other children his age, then the sitting time may suit the child. If the child is a reluctant or disabled reader, has difficulty paying attention in school, or is uncomfortable with the issues in the book, you may need to consider even shorter sessions. For these shorter sessions, use the 'tired turtle' symbol to let you know when would be a good time for a break. The 'tired turtle' appears within the sub-sections. The point at which you see the 'tired turtle' is a good place to stop if the child is showing signs of fatigue or frustration. The next time you sit down to work on the book you can begin where you left off.

While actually completing the sub-section with your child you will need to be sensitive to the nonverbal cues he or she unconsciously gives to you. Signs of frustration (fidgeting, frequent sighing, whining, crying, getting up and down, constant turning to other pages, closing the book, refusal to continue, complaining about the topics, not wanting to get started each time) should be met with understanding and should signal you to stop work immediately. Conscious signals, such as refusing to go on, should also tell you to stop.

Working on *FILLING IN THE BLANKS* should be a positive experience for the child if at all possible. You will find that letting the child's behavior show you how much he can tolerate leads to quality times together. If you don't force the amount of time, if you let the child work for as long (or as little) as the child is able, you may find that the child is comfortable about the time spent together.

If, however, you find that the child is not able to work on the book *at all*, you might consider consulting with others about possible reasons for this. It is possible that some of the issues in the book will cause emotional strain. With the help of others you may be able to look for ways to approach these issues that will lessen the strain. If you find that dealing with some issues raised in *FILLING IN THE BLANKS* does indeed cause emotional strain, you may want to ask a helping professional to work on the book with you and with your child. Most parents, with a little help, should be able to enjoy the book with their children. This leads us to the next question.

2. Is a parent able to work through the book with a child or should a professional be the one to do it?

This, too, is a good question. Traditionally, adoption and foster care workers have been the ones to work with children with books similar to this. These books have been called "lifebooks". However, many adoptive families have not had this kind of preparation and support before adoption. Many adoption and foster care workers report that although they are told to do lifebooks with children, they are given no guidelines, nothing written to follow.

The answer to whether a parent and child should work alone or get extra help probably depends upon both the child's needs and abilities and the parent's. If adoption was smooth, the child is secure, and the parent is sensitive and understanding as well as willing to seek help if needed, then parent and child starting this book on their own can be a positive option. If, the adoption had difficulties, the child has some problem areas, or the parent feels a strong need for assistance, then help from other parents or professionals can be very useful. Someone other than the parent may also work with the child if this is needed.

Although parent and child completing the book together is the preferable method, it is recognized that some families won't feel comfortable in doing so. In that case, it is more preferable to let a professional work with the child on *FILLING IN THE BLANKS.* than not to use this book. When a professional does work with the child, the more the family can get involved, the better. One of the tasks of the professional is to help parent and child to work on at least some of *FILLING IN THE BLANKS* together.

3. How should I handle the 'Birth Roots' section if I can't find any information about my child's birth family? What do I do if I have negative information about my child's birth family?

A very common concern with adoptive families is the birth family. Some people who were adopted and their parents choose to ignore the birth family. Or, they may change or hide information. However, that is unwise. Honesty about the past and present is always the healthiest way to live.

If you diligently search for any information at all and can find little or nothing, you must be honest with your child. Many children who were adopted from other countries know nothing of their birth history and never will. They must learn to deal with this unknown gap in their lives. Completing the BIRTH FAMILY section can help them to do that. Even if you know nothing about a child's birth family, this section deals with that and with the emotions caused by those unanswered questions.

One good reason to purchase *FILLING IN THE BLANKS* before your adoption is that it will help you to know what information you need from your adoption worker. Sometimes, adoption workers have access to more information about the birth family than they share with adoptive families. They may be concerned about your ability to deal with the information, or they may think you don't want to know. However, more workers are realizing the importance of openness with adoptive families. Nevertheless, knowing what to ask is extremely helpful during the adoption process. Afterwards, if you have lost contact with that adoption worker, or the records have been sealed by the courts, you may not be able to obtain the information.

If you have little information about the birth family and you are honest with yourself and your child, you may be able to find ways to express the sensitive, honest, caring words needed. (Adoption workers or other adoptive parents can help here.) If you don't know why adoption was chosen for your child, then you must say just that. An additional explanation about how difficult it is when we don't know answers to important questions would then be in order.

Yet, even if you are honest and positive with the child, you may find some explanations difficult and some thoughts hard to express. This is understandable, since adoption issues can sometimes be difficult to discuss. Again, you can be honest about your difficulty, and seek guidance from people you trust.

If you feel that what you know about birth parents or other parts of the child's life would be negative or damaging to the child at the time, then *don't lie*. Spend some time thinking of a sensitive way to deal with the issue. Talk with helping professionals and other adoptive parents before working on that section or sub-section. If your child already knows negative information and is unable to discuss this topic, think about letting a professional help. Sometimes talking with other children who have similar experiences can be helpful, too. There may be formal or informal contacts that can be made. Try a local adoptive parent group, an adoption or foster care worker or other helping professional who knows about adoption.

Planning Guide

By now you are probably ready to make some decisions about how to proceed. You now need to thoroughly read the rest of the book. Pay special attention to the glossary at the end. The glossary can help you to understand the words that the child will find in this book. Some of these words are familiar, but you may find them defined differently in *FILLING IN THE BLANKS*. Some of these words are new. They can better help you to understand adoption issues.

Plan to use the glossary as needed while you are working on the book. It can be especially helpful when you are working on the sections out of order. If you come to a word that was explained in a section you haven't done yet, you can look it up in the glossary.

Once you have done this reading you will need to ask yourself the following questions. These questions will help you decide how you need to plan for this project.

1. Which method or combination of methods for use is best for my child?
   a. Sequential use?
   b. Need-oriented use?
   c. Child determined use?
   d. Birth/arrival to adolesence use?
   e. Combination of some of the above? Which ones?

2. Which adult or combination of adults will use the book?
   a. Parent and child alone?
   b. Parent and child with helping professional?
   c. Child with helping professional?
   d. Parent and child with teacher?
   e. Combination of some of the above? Which ones?

3. Is my child a reluctant or disabled reader? If so, what will I do to gain help in planning for my child?
   a. Who will I contact?
   b. Will I use teachers or other professionals to help complete the project?
   c. Do I know other parents with children who have similar needs? Could they help?
   d. At what age or stage will my child be ready for this project?
   e. What changes will I need to make in the length of time spent in one sitting?
   f. What changes will I need to make in the writing activities?
   g. Are there any other things I need to consider?

4. Does my child have difficulty with some of the issues in this book?
   a. If so, where will I seek help?
   b. What might some of the difficulties be?
   c. Which particular sections might be difficult?
   d. How can I approach these sections so that my child is able to deal with these issues?

Now it is time for you to **TEAR OUT THESE INTRODUCTORY PAGES** so that you can keep them for yourself. *FILLING IN THE BLANKS* is your child's book and should not contain these adult-oriented pages. Once your plans are complete, if and when your child is ready for this book, then you are ready to begin this exciting project with your child! But remember, begin only when you feel both of you are ready. And enjoy!

FILLING IN THE BLANKS

A Guided Look at
Growing Up Adopted

by Susan Gabel

Illustrations by Julie Seregny

Perspectives Press
Indianapolis, Indiana

Perspectives Press
P. O. Box 90318
Indianapolis, Indiana 46290-0318

Manufactured in the United States of America
ISBN 0-9609504-8-6

To my children— Bobby, Tiffany, April, and Benjamin— who "taught" me what an adoption story is all about. And to the birth child who never came, who made room for more "teachers".

ACKNOWLEDGEMENTS

My deepest appreciation must go to many people who, jointly and singly, have made this book possible.

Thanks, Mom and Dad, for introducing me to adoption stories by adopting Kim and Debbie. Growing up in an adoptive family has meant so much to me. It instilled in me attitudes about family life, love, and commitment for which I'll always be grateful. Kim and Debbie taught me the happy and the sad things that can be part of adoption. Today they are grown with families of their own. I think they've even reached acceptance of their adoption stories and their own many unanswered questions. Perhaps one of the most important things they've given to me has been an understanding of the often intense struggle to accept the fact that unanswered questions may forever be part of life.

My husband, Peter, has weathered many storms in these last six years. He has loved me in spite of many day-after-all-nighters-working-on-the-book grouchies. He's learned about adoption stories first hand as we together have formed our family by adoption. He's cared for our children more than his share as I sat typing away at my manuscript. He's been thrilled and frustrated along with me as either a publisher showed interest or an editor's fell swoop struck for the third or fourth time. Thanks, Peter, for seeing the good this book could do and for encouraging me all the way. Thanks for putting much of our life on hold for so long until this book was done!

My four children truly are the motivation and inspiration for this work. They have grown and changed through our family's adoption stories. They have been my greatest joy. Six years ago I began looking for a book like this to share with our oldest son, Bob. I never found the book I wanted, so I began to write what I wanted to share with him. Needless to say, the years have ticked by and Bob is older now. He'll get the first copy when it's ready! Thanks, Bob, for showing me the need for this book. You are my first child and my first teacher. I love you for that.

Thanks to little Tiffany, too, who has taught me so much about adjustment and its difficulties as well as the rewards of sticking it out to the end. Our adjustment problems after Tiffy arrived were no fault of hers, but rather, my own shortcomings. Thanks for sticking it out with your mom, Tiffy. I'm so glad you did!

I owe our little April a lot of thanks for this book, too. She has shown me the path to openness in adoption. We talk about her birth mother and father, what they might look like, where they might live. Sometimes she looks for them when we are out together. Her birth family tugs strongly at her heart at times. I'm so happy to have learned openness from you, April.

And Benjamin, my youngest child from Korea, what a wonderful teacher you have been! You have taught me the joy of immediate and unquestioning bonding. You have been my answered prayer. Little Ben, first experiencing family at age four, I'm so proud to be your mom.

Naturally, this book could not have been polished nor published without the wise eyes of an editor who could look beyond the rough draft and into the future of a book with potential. My editor's passion for adoption stories and concern for this haggard author has kept me going through many difficult revisions. Warm appreciation must go to Pat Johnston, senior editor at Perspectives. Pat has spent many long hours on the phone with me, revising and refining. I owe her everything for this opportunity.

Another person to whom I owe much is Joan McNamara. Her careful, sensitive editing added just the right touch to this final product. With her knowledge of many different adoption stories, this book is more flexible and will be more helpful to families.

Finally, I must surprise a very special adoption worker with a very special acknowledgement. Julia Smith, our social worker through our first three adoptions, highly skilled professional, and long-distance friend and confidant, thank you! Julia was the first person to see the very first draft of this book six years ago. Julia was the first person to hear that the book had been accepted by Perspectives Press. Thank you, Julia, for having faith in me and in this work. Thank you for encouraging me to write the book and to continue searching for a publisher. You're the best!

Susan Gabel
Southfield, Michigan
February, 1988

Table of Contents

HOW TO USE YOUR BOOK

You were adopted. You may have some questions and feelings about adoption going around in your head. Do you ever wonder why you were adopted? Do you feel happy to have your parents? Do you sometimes think about your birth mother and father? Do you want to remember the important things that have happened to you? Do you want to talk with someone about being adopted? These questions and many more are part of your life story. The answers to questions are also part of your story. Everything that has happened to you because of your adoption is part of your life story. And your future will be part of your adoption story.

To use this book you will need the help of an adult. This adult will help you find answers and talk about them. The adult can share feelings with you. This adult can help you to learn as much about your life story as possible. Your adult helper may be a parent. You and your family may decide that you want to ask another adult for help. If you do that, your adult helper may sometimes be someone who understands adoption and can help you with parts of your life story that may feel uncomfortable.

Some of the things in *FILLING IN THE BLANKS* may be exciting to do. Other things will take courage from you to finish. But you can finish this book if you work slowly and surely. Take breaks. Don't get discouraged. Ask for help from family and friends. Ask for help from other people who were adopted. Ask for help from an adult who understands adoption.

Before you begin work on your book, you will need to read the introduction to each section with the adult who is helping you. As you read, you can decide together which parts of your book to complete first and which can wait. By reading the introduction to each section, you can learn a little of what each section is about. This way you will be better able to make decisions about how you will work on your book.

You don't have to work on your book from beginning to end. You can start in the middle if you and the adult helping you decide that is best. You can move from the end of one section to the beginning of any other section. You and the adult helping you are the ones to make those decisions. It's important to do a whole section in order after you've decided to work on it. Start at the beginning of the section and work to the end of it.

If you choose to do your sections out of order, you may need to use the glossary. If you read some words that you don't understand, you may be able to find them in the glossary. Using the glossary can help you understand each section without doing them in order.

Each section of *FILLING IN THE BLANKS* is divided into smaller parts called sub-sections. You will know when a new sub-section begins when you see a sunrise with a numeral inside the sun. It will look like this. The sunrise is a sign to you that this is a new topic.

As you complete each section, there will be some reading, some thinking, some talking, and some writing for you to do. The adult helping you will do these things with you. Each section will start with some words to talk about. After you talk about the words, you can read something about adoption. Then you can write about your own adoption. Sometimes the writing is fill-in-the-blank. Other times it is a letter or a poem. There are many different writing choices in your book.

At times you may find that you become too tired to finish a section that you have begun. Or, you may find that some writing is not for you because it is not part of your adoption story. Three picture symbols in your book can help you when these things happen.

One symbol you will see is the "TIRED TURTLE". It will look like this. When you see the turtle, it means "TAKE A REST". The "TIRED TURTLE" will appear in places that are good resting points, if you find yourself getting tired while working on your book. When you see this symbol, feel free to put your book away until another time. Of course, you don't have to "TAKE A REST" unless you need one!

Another symbol that you will find is a "JUMPING FROG". It will look like this. When you see the frog, it means "JUMP AHEAD". This symbol will usually appear when there is writing to do. If the writing isn't part of your adoption story you can "JUMP AHEAD" to the next part which may again be part of your adoption story.

Once you have jumped ahead, you may wonder where to begin again. You can know where to jump toward by looking for the frog's "LILY PAD". It will look like this. When you see this symbol, you can begin reading again. The "LILY PAD" is the third symbol you can find in your book. It tells you to "LAND HERE" when you are "JUMPING AHEAD".

As you work on your book, you may choose to do sections that are important to you first. If you do this, the adult can help you know what to do. If you choose to do your book out of order, it can be best to use the glossary in the back of your book. When you read a word that you don't understand, look for it in your glossary.

This book is about you. It is your own autobiography in a way. It's about the families in your life. It's about the way you were adopted and why. It's about the person you are now and the person you are becoming. You probably have some thoughts about your life story. You may wonder why you were adopted. You may want to know or remember important things that have happened to you. You might not have had the chance to talk with someone about being adopted. Your book can help you sort through some of this, because it is about you and for you.

There are many writers of your life's story. Your story was started by the adults who made adoption plans for you. Your family, too, helped to write it by adopting you. But the most important person in your story is you. You are the most important character. You can also be the most important writer of your story. Your book can help you to be your own story writer.

Now it is time to begin *FILLING IN THE BLANKS*. First, read the introduction to each section with the adult helping you. Then, decide where you will begin. Good luck!

MY BIRTH FAMILY

Every story has a set of characters. The people in your birth family are some of the characters in your life's story. The events that you share with them are part of your adoption story, too. In this section you can think about these beginnings of your story. Where did you live when your story began? Who is in your birth family and can you find out what they look like? Do you look like them? Do you have birth brothers and sisters? Where are they? These are all questions that you may or may not be able to answer now.

You can also think about your birth parents in this section. Everyone has two birth parents. These are the two people who give life to a baby. Our birth parents are part of a larger birth family. The birth family is made up of all the relatives that are related to us by birth. Some people live with their birth families all through childhood. Other people are born to a birth family and later live with an adoptive family.

People who were adopted start life with their birth family like everybody else. But since they become part of an adoptive family, it may not be easy to see or feel what that start was like, because they may not see or know their birth family. Sometimes it can be painful to think about your birth family. Some people who were adopted find that it really hurts. Others have spent some time thinking and feeling and have come to accept it all as part of their life.

The adult working with you can help you with these questions and feelings. The adult can work with you by looking for information about your birth family. Your adult helper can talk with you, listen to you, share with you about your birth family. Now you can begin *FILLING IN THE BLANKS* . . . together.

1 QUESTIONS ABOUT BIRTH PARENTS

Before you go on, please talk about these important words with the adult helping you.

Nurture means to take care of, to help to grow, to train, to teach. Children are nurtured by parents so that they can grow up healthy and happy.

Birth Parents are the mother and father who give life to a baby. Everyone has a birth mother and father. Some people are nurtured by their birth parents. Other people are nurtured by their adoptive parents.

Adoptive Parents are mothers and fathers who choose to nurture a child they did not give birth to.

One thing everyone has in common is that we all have a birth mother and father. Some of us are always taken care of by our **birth parents**. Others are born to a birth mother and father, and then are **nurtured** by **adoptive parents**.

Many people who were adopted think about their birth mothers and birth fathers. It's OK to think about them. Do you ever think about your birth parents? Do you think about anyone else in your birth family? Do you have questions about them?

Asking questions is a good way to learn about yourself. Questions can help you look for answers. They can also point to those answers that will not come. Questions are a good way to begin to accept your birth family as a part of your life.

Below are some questions you might have. There's room for you to add your own questions if you don't find them all here. Later, you can look back at these questions to see which ones you have been able to answer by working on your book. For now you might put a check beside the questions you would like answered.

____ What do my birth parents look like?

____ Were they married?

____ How old were my birth parents when I was born?

____ Where did they live when I was born?

____ Where do my birth parents live now?

____ What do my birth parents look like?

____ Do I look like my birth parents?

____ Whom do I look like the most?

____ Do I have any birth brothers or sisters?

____ If so, where do they live?

____ Why were adoption plans made for me?

____ Who made those plans?

____ How do I feel about being adopted?

____ (Other) _____

____ (Other) _____

____ (Other) _____

____ (Other) _____

____ (Other) _____

# 2 WHAT BIRTH PARENTS LOOK LIKE

Some people who were adopted wonder what their birth parents look like. Some knew their birth parents and can remember what they look like. Other people have pictures of them. But many people cannot remember their birth parents and do not have pictures of them. This is especially true if people were adopted when they were very little.

It can be difficult to not know much about birth parents. That's a normal problem. Many people have difficulty with questions that can never be fully answered.

If you don't know what your birth parents look like, then you could imagine what they might look like. You could close your eyes and imagine their hair, their skin, their faces. You could imagine their shape and their size. You could imagine the expression on their faces.

Let's put that picture of your birth parents here. You can use this space to write or to draw what you remember or imagine. If you have a photo, you can use that.

3 WHY ADOPTION?

Before you go on, please talk about this important word with the adult helping you.

> **Adoption** is the choice that adults make when parents cannot be nurturing parents for their children. This is when adoptive parents become the nurturing parents.

There are lots of reasons why **adoption** is chosen for children. Some birth parents may not be ready to be parents. They may be very young or all alone. They may have a lot of hurt in their lives that needs to heal. Birth mothers or fathers may have problems that make it hard for them to take on the responsibilities of being a parent.

You may or may not know why adoption was chosen for you. The choice was made, though, so that you would have the best chance of growing up strong and loved. If you know why adoption was chosen for you, you can write that reason here. Ask the adult to help you with the words if you feel you need help.

_____

_____

_____

_____

_____

_____

_____

_____

_____

_____

_____

_____

All stories have titles. A title tells us the most important message in a story. Your life story could have a title. At different times in your story, or at different times in your life, you might give it a different title. If you could choose a title for your story right now, what would it be? Choose one of the titles below, or make up your own.

____ Adoption is for Me   ____ Why Was I Adopted?

____ Where are the Answers?   ____ Happiness is . . .

____ My Adoption Story   ____ Loneliness is . . .

____ Where Are My Birth Parents? ____ (Other) _____

If you don't know why adoption was chosen for you, then you are like many people who were adopted. That is one part of your life you may not have the answer to now. It may be a long time before you can find that answer. Or, the answer may never come. Just like other unanswered questions, you may find this difficult to accept at first. But your adoptive family may be able to help you find answers when you are an adult if the answers are hard to get now.

Some people who don't know why adoption was chosen for them imagine the reasons. This can make them feel better. Can you imagine the reasons adoption plans might have been made for you? What do you imagine?

_____

_____

_____

How do you feel about not having much information? _____

_____

_____

_____

When you are an adult, would you like your adoptive parents to help you find these answers? Why or why not? _____

_____

_____

_____

_____

4 BIRTH BROTHERS AND SISTERS

Before you go on, please talk about this important word with the adult helping you.

> **Siblings** are brothers or sisters related by birth or by adoption. Birth siblings are brothers or sisters related by birth. These brothers or sisters may share both the same father and mother, or they may share one parent. If they share one parent it could be either the same mother or the same father.

Do you have brothers or sisters in your family? There may be brothers or sisters in your birth family too. You may have lived together at one time or maybe you never met. Adoption workers try to find one adoptive family for all birth **siblings** who need a home. They try to do this so the brothers or sisters can still be together. Sometimes this is possible. Sometimes it is not. When birth siblings must be in different families, they may write letters or call or visit one another. Sometimes they may not do this, though. They may not even know or remember each other.

Here you can write what you might know about your birth siblings.

Birth Brothers' Names and Ages _____

_____

Where They Live _____

Birth Sisters' Names and Ages _____

_____

Where They Live _____

If your birth siblings don't live with you, you may not know much about them. Even if they have birth siblings, many people who were adopted don't know much about theirs. This is especially true if they were adopted when they were very little. That's another question that may be answered when you are older. Or it may never be answered. There are many of those questions, aren't there? Perhaps you'd like to write about what you wish you knew about your birth brothers and sisters. You can ask an adult to help you.

_____

_____

_____

_____

_____

_____

_____

_____

_____

_____

_____

_____

_____

_____

_____

_____

_____

_____

_____

_____

_____

_____

5 HOW DO I FEEL?

Before you go on, please talk about this important word with the adult helping you.

Mixed Feelings are when people have more than one feeling at the same time. Sometimes these different feelings are opposite feelings and happen all at the same time. This can make a person feel confused. Sometimes different feelings come and go one at a time. Sometimes these different feelings aren't easy to put your finger on and they make a person feel sad without knowing why. Mixed feelings sometimes make it hard to want to think about whatever gives us mixed feelings.

People who were adopted can have many different feelings about their birth parents. That's okay. Some people haven't thought about their birth parents much. That's okay too. Some people feel sad or angry. Some people remember their birth parents with love. Most people have **mixed feelings**. These mixed feelings might be sadness and excitement at the same time. Or, they might be anger and love at the same time. Or a person could feel happy one minute and a little sad the next.

Having mixed feelings sometimes makes people feel confused. Have you ever felt confused? Do you ever have mixed feelings? Have you ever worried about how you feel? These are all part of being adopted. In fact, they are part of being a person. Everyone experiences these feelings sometimes. It's okay to have mixed feelings, confusion, and worries.

It can help to share your feelings with the adult helping you. You may also want to write about your feelings first, and then talk about them. Or you could talk first and then write them down.

Here are some sentences that will help you to get started. See if you can finish all of them.

When I think about my birth parents I feel _____

_____

When I imagine how my birth mother looks I imagine her _____

_____

Every time I think about being adopted I feel _____

_____

If people could see me when I'm all alone and thinking about my birth family I
would look _____

_____

When I tell people I was adopted, it seems like _____

_____

If I could choose to be adopted or not, I would choose _____

_____

Sometimes I wish _____

_____

Many nights I _____

_____

Often I have wondered _____

_____

If I could meet my birth father I would _____

_____

_____

_____

If I saw my birth mother I would _____

_____

_____

_____

If we lived together my birth family and I would _____

_____

_____

_____

_____

_____

_____

_____

_____

Now here is space for you to write some more. It can be anything you want. Perhaps you would like to write a poem to someone in your birth family. Or maybe you'd like to write a letter to someone. You could write a song about how you feel about your adoption if you like music. Ask for help if you need it.

_____

_____

_____

_____

_____

_____

_____

_____

_____

_____

_____

_____

_____

_____

_____

_____

_____

_____

_____

_____

_____

_____

_____

_____

_____

_____

6 INHERITED TRAITS

Before you go on, please talk about this important word with the adult helping you.

> **Inherited Traits** are physical or health patterns, talents, and preferences that people have even before birth. Inherited traits come from birth parents, grandparents, and other birth ancestors.

Everyone **inherits traits** from their birth parents. Physical traits are things like hair color, skin color, height, and some health patterns. Other inherited traits might be talents, interests, emotional make-up, and personality.

Sometimes adoption workers and adoptive parents don't know what traits birth parents give their children. Sometimes children who were adopted may know what health problems run in their birth families. Sometimes, only the child's birth weight and height are known. Some children don't know anything about what they inherited from their birth parents because there is no birth family information available at all.

It's important to know our inherited traits if possible, because certain health problems and diseases can be inherited. There are some problems we can treat best if we know about them before they happen. A few problems that may be inherited are nearsightedness, alcoholism, heart disease, high blood pressure. There are many others. If you can find out about your birth family's inherited traits you can have more information to keep yourself healthy.

Adoption workers are beginning to understand that people who were adopted need to know a lot more about their birth parents. So, they're trying to get as much information as possible before adoptions take place or before records are closed. After records are closed it can be very difficult to get information about a birth family. Adoption workers may be able to share this information with you or your adoptive parents.

You may look different from your adoptive parents or you may look like them. But since your physical traits come from your birth parents, you probably look a little like someone in your birth family. If you know some of your birth parents' physical traits, or if you can imagine what they are, you can write them on the next page.

This is what I know about what my birth mother looks like _____

_____

These are the health problems that we know run in her family _____

_____

These are her talents and interests _____

_____

This is what I know about what my birth father looks like _____

_____

These are health problems that we know run in his family _____

_____

These are his talents and interests _____

_____

Physical traits that I might have inherited from my birth parents _____

_____

_____

Other traits or talents I might have inherited from my birth parents _____

_____

_____

_____

    If you don't have information about your birth parents, perhaps you'd like to use this space to write about what you imagine them to be like.

_____

_____

_____

_____

_____

_____

_____

_____

_____

_____

_____

MY ADOPTION PROCESS

Each story has a main event. The main event in your adoption story is your adoption! Although your adoption actually happened a while ago, you may still be feeling like it's not quite over. This is because adoption, like any relationship, can take time to work out. The adoption process includes everything that takes place from the moment adoption plans are started until you and your adoptive family have adjusted and are living together because you very much want to be together. This can take years for some families. Other families complete this process in a few months.

The very first step in the adoption process is planning. Everyone who was adopted had an adoption plan. The people who made adoption choices for you, the choices they made, when and how your adoption took place are all part of your adoption plan. These adoption plans are part of the adoption process. They were made for you by adults who wanted you to grow up in a family that could meet your needs. The next few sections of your book can help you to understand the different kinds of adoption plans and which ones describe your adoption.

There are other parts of the adoption process, too. There are certain ways that most adoptions must take place. Laws and rules control some parts of the adoption process. These are to protect children and families. Another part of the adoption process involves where the child lives before the adoption and who helps with the adoption. Finalization (finishing the legal papers of the adoption) is also part of the adoption process.

Learning to live together as a family is part of the adoption process. This part of the process is called adjustment. You can learn about adjustment in this section of your book.

Each adoption process is different because each child and family is different. It is important to understand about yours so that you can better understand yourself and your family. This part of your book can help you find out more about how your adoption happened. It can also help you to understand what your adoption meant to everyone in your family.

As you begin to understand your adoption process, you may find that you better understand your adoption story, too. You can also learn a lot about yourself and your family if you learn about your adoption process. This section will help you with these things.

1 AN INTRODUCTION TO THE ADOPTION PROCESS

Before you go on, please talk about these important words with the adult helping you.

Adopt is to legally join one or more parents and a child who was not born to them to make a family.

Adoption Laws are rules made by a government about adoption. These can be different from place to place.

Adoption Process is the way an adoption happens to make a new family.

Adoption Worker is the adult who helps children and parents come together as a family. This adult may also work with families after a child enters the family through adoption.

Each **adoption** that is planned has certain things that happen to make the plan work for the child and the family. The way an adoption happens is called an **adoption process**.

In most countries there are **adoption laws** that give rules about the adoption process. These rules protect the rights of children, birth parents, and adoptive parents. There are many ways an adoption can happen. Your adoption process may be different from your friend's, even if you came from the same place at the same time. But all adoptions must follow the rules of the place where the adoption happens.

After a child moves into an adoptive family an **adoption worker** must make sure everything is done according to the rules. This adoption worker may also help the family to grow together. A lawyer will also help the family with these rules and with the papers for the court. Papers must be completed so that the adoption will be permanent according to the law.

2 WHY ADOPT?

Before going on, please talk about these important words with the adult helping you.

Adoptive Family is the family that adopts. It can be made up of one parent, or two parents, and one or more children who were adopted. It can have children who were born into the family also.

Adoption Choices are the decisions and plans that adults make for children who need adoptive parents. Or, they are the decisions that adults make to become adoptive parents.

There are lots of reasons why families adopt children. The main reason is that an adult has love to share with a child. This adult enjoys helping children grow within a family. Sometimes when an adult has this love to share and enjoys children in a family, the adult makes an **adoption choice**. This adoption choice is to be come an **adoptive family**.

There are other reasons a family might decide to adopt. Some families have children born to them but want to love another child who needs a home. Some families are not able to have children born to them, so they adopt. This may be the only way they can have children. Some families have no children yet and decide that adoption is the way to start their families. Other families meet a boy or girl who needs a family and then adopt that child because they grow to love the child. Whatever the reason, adoptive families want and love their children very much.

Have you ever asked your parents why they chose to adopt? If not, now is a good time to do that. Here is space for you to write their answer.

My family chose adoption because _____

_____

_____

_____

_____

_____

Part of the adoption choice is saying yes to a certain child. Your family said yes to you. They made the choice to adopt you instead of another child. Have you ever asked your family why they chose to adopt you instead of someone else? Now is a good time to ask. Write the answers here.

My family chose to adopt me because _____

_____

_____

_____

_____

_____

_____

_____

_____

_____

_____

_____

There are many adoption choices that families must make and many reasons for these choices. Knowing the reasons why your family chose adoption and chose to adopt you can help you to understand your adoption story a little better.

HOW I FEEL

Everyone who was adopted has feelings about being adopted. Feelings about adoption can range from being happy about a loving family to being sad about not being with birth parents. Some adopted children even sometimes wonder if their adoptive families really love them! (Children who grow up in their birth homes often wonder about this too!)

It is important for you to know that all of your feelings about being adopted are okay. Feelings cannot be bad. What you do about those feelings can be good or bad for you. You should realize how you feel. If you are mostly happy about being adopted, then that's good for you. Share that happiness with your family. If you are mostly sad about it, you can talk about that with your family or another adult. Working through that sadness can make you happier. Here is where you can write how you feel about being adopted. First you can finish some feeling sentences, then you can write whatever you want about your feelings.

When I think about my birth parents I feel _____

_____

_____

If I ever met my birth parents I would _____

_____

Sometimes, when I'm alone, I think about _____

_____

If people ask me about my birth family I say _____

_____

When I think about birth brothers and sisters I _____

_____

_____

If I had to describe my feelings in one word it would be _____

_____

If I could give the birth family part of my adoption story a title, it would be _____

_____

When I think about my adoptive family and my birth family both at the same time I _____

_____

Here is how I feel about being adopted

_____

_____

_____

_____

_____

_____

_____

_____

_____

_____

_____

Sometimes there are certain times or events that make a child who was adopted especially happy or sad about being adopted. These are part of having mixed feelings too. Many people who were adopted have mixed feelings about it at different times in their lives. Does this happen to you? When? You can write your thoughts here.

The time that I feel most sad about not seeing my birth family is when _____

_____

The time that I think the most about my birth family is _____

_____

The thing that makes me happiest about being adopted is _____

_____

The thing that can make me sad about being adopted is _____

_____

This is something people say to me about adoption that hurts my feelings

_____

_____

4 AGENCY ADOPTIONS IN THIS COUNTRY

Before going on, please talk about these important words with the adult helping you.

Adoption Agency is the place that brings together children who need families with families who need children.

Agency Adoption is an adoption planned with the help of an adoption agency. This agency can be a public one run by a city, county, state or other government department. Or, the agency can be a private one which has permission to plan adoptions, but is not run by the government.

Adoption Study is the way an agency learns about a family that has chosen adoption. It is also the way a family can learn more about the adoption choices it must make. During the adoption study, a family may spend time with an adoption worker and other adoptive families, talking and learning about children who need families.

There are many plans that must be made during an **agency adoption** process. The first plan is often which **adoption agency** to choose. Families that choose agency adoptions choose between public and private ones. The adoption agency must follow all the laws and rules of adoption when making adoption plans for a child. Did your family have the help of an agency to adopt you? If so, which kind of agency did your family choose? Do you still see anyone from the agency? If yours was an agency adoption, you can write down this information here.

Name of agency: _____

Address of agency: _____

_____

Phone number of agency: _____

Why your family chose an agency adoption: _____

_____

_____

The name of your adoption worker: _____

Before an agency brings together a child and a family, other plans must be made. The agency must know as much as possible about the child to decide what kind of family would be best for the child. The agency wants a family to meet a child's needs. All children share the same needs for clothing, shelter, food, and love. But other needs can be different from child to child.

If the child is older, the agency must prepare the child for adoption. For this, an adoption worker may talk and share with the child to help the child understand what it means to be part of an adoptive family.

Do you know what kind of plans were made for your adoption? Who helped to make your adoption plans? Why was your family chosen for you? If you were an older child, how did your adoption worker prepare you for the adoption? Here is space for you to write about these adoption plans.

My agency wanted a family for me that would _____

_____

_____

The people that helped to make these adoption plans for me were _____

_____

_____

This is how long it took for my adoption plans to be made _____

_____

(If you were an older child . . .)

The people that helped to prepare me for my adoption were _____

_____

This is how they helped to prepare me _____

_____

_____

_____

The adoption agency and the family must make some plans together. An **adoption study** is the planning that they do together so the family can learn about themselves, adoption, and about children who need families. This adoption study can be done with an adoption worker and sometimes with other adoptive parents. The things they learn can help them to make good adoption choices. Sometimes people do this studying and decide that adoption is not the best choice for them.

When the work is complete, the adoption worker, or the parents, or both may write a report about their choices. This report can help the agency to bring the child together with the family that can best meet the child's needs.

Many people choose an agency adoption because they want the help of someone who understands adoption. An agency can give this help. You can ask your family what kind of plans they made with their adoption agency. Write what you learn here.

_____

_____

_____

_____

_____

_____

_____

_____

_____

_____

_____

_____

_____

_____

_____

_____

5 ADOPTION WITHOUT AN AGENCY IN THIS COUNTRY

Before you go on, please talk about this important word with the adult helping you.

> **Independent Adoption** is an adoption planned without the help of an adoption agency.

Many children were adopted through **independent adoption**. Most (but not all) children adopted this way are babies. In an independent adoption, the birth parents and the adoptive parents do not use an agency. They may never meet. But in a way they are together making adoption plans for this child. Sometimes the birth family and the adoptive family contact one another directly to make adoption plans. This is called openness in adoption.

Other times someone else helps these two families with the adoption plans. Then, the families may or may not meet during the adoption process. This helping person may be a relative, friend, clergyperson, lawyer, doctor, children's home director, or another adult. Sometimes people call an independent adoption a "private adoption". But this is not the same as an adoption with a private agency.

Even though this kind of adoption is not planned by an agency, adoption laws and rules must still be followed. After a child joins a family through an independent adoption, an adoption worker must meet with the family to make sure the family is growing together. A lawyer must help with this kind of adoption, too.

If yours was an independent adoption, you can write about it here. Ask your family for help.

My family chose an independent adoption because _____

_____

_____

The people who helped make my adoption plans are _____

_____

_____

This is how long it took to make my adoption plans _____

_____

_____

When my family first heard about me and decided to adopt me they _____

_____

_____

_____

_____

_____

_____

_____

_____

(If your birth parents and adoptive parents met and planned together . . .)

When my birth parents and adoptive parents planned together they _____

_____

_____

_____

_____

_____

When they met they talked about _____

_____

_____

_____

_____

_____

_____

_____

_____

_____

6 INTERNATIONAL ADOPTIONS

Before you go on, please talk about these important words with the adult helping you.

International Adoption is an adoption which brings together a child from one country who needs a family with a family from another country who needs a child.

Birth Country is the country where a person is born.

Birth Language is the language of the country where a person is born.

An **international adoption** can be either an agency or an independent adoption. An international agency adoption may be with the help of agencies in one or both of the countries. In some countries only agency adoptions are allowed. (You may want to go back to pages 22 - 26 and read about agency and independent adoptions in this country before you go on. Reading those pages will help you understand a little more about these two kinds of international adoptions.)

An international independent adoption would need the help of a lawyer, friend, birth family, children's home director, or another adult. In some countries there are no agencies. The only way to plan an adoption with these countries is with the help of another adult in an independent adoption.

In other countries, both types of adoptions are possible. No matter what kind of adoption it is, adoption laws must be followed. There are adoption laws in the child's **birth country**, and laws in the adoptive family's country. There are two rules that are almost always followed. One is that the child must get permission from his or her birth country to be able to leave for the adoption. Another is that the adoptive family must get permission from their country for their child to enter the country for adoption.

These rules can be very confusing and paperwork for following rules can take a long time. Sometimes, there is not a long wait and the adoption can be quick. Every adoption is different, as you have learned.

If yours was an international adoption, you may want to find out as much as you can about it. Ask your family to help you. (If some of your paperwork is in your **birth language**, you may need the help of someone who can read that language!)

My adoption was an (circle one) agency / independent one.
The people making my adoption plans were _____
_____

My birth country is _____
I was born in the city of _____
My name in my birth language is _____
My adoption plans took this long _____
When my family was told about me, this is what they learned _____
_____
_____
_____

Here is what I looked like when my family got the first photo of me: (draw a picture or use a photo)

A child who was adopted internationally usually travels long distances to get to the new family. Sometimes the child has an adult on the trip to help. This helper is called an escort. The escort helps the child eat and use the bathroom, talks to the child, and comforts the child. Sometimes the escort is helping several children at the same time. When the child has reached the place where the family will meet the child, the escort may also introduce them.

An older child coming such a long way from the birth country may have some special worries about the adoption. The child might worry about never seeing the birth country or hearing the birth language again. The child may worry about being different from the adoptive family. Or, the child may worry that the new family won't understand the language and won't know what the child needs or wants. These worries are all normal. Many children have them. Even children who do not travel from other countries have these worries. With help and hard work, most families are able to work through these things and live together successfully. Now you can write something about your trip to your new country.

I came to my new country by _____

The trip took this long _____

The people that helped me during the trip were _____

_____

The first thing I thought when I got to my new country was _____

_____

When my family was waiting for me to arrive, they _____

_____

_____

_____

_____

These are the things that I was concerned about (use your imagination if you don't remember) _____

_____

_____

_____

_____

7 WHERE CHILDREN LIVE BEFORE ADOPTION

Before going on, please talk about these important words with the adult helping you.

Foster Home is a home where some children are cared for when they cannot be with their birth families. Some children live in foster homes before adoption.

Foster Parent is the person who cares for the child in a foster home.

Children's Home is a place where many children live who cannot live with their birth families. Here, they are cared for by many adults. Other names for a children's home are residence, children's center, orphanage. Some children's homes have special care for children who need help with special problems they may have.

Birth Home is the home in which the birth mother and/or father live. The child may or may not have lived there before the adoption.

Children can live in many different places before adoption. Some children are in their **birth homes** before living in a **foster home** or being adopted. If they are older when the adoption choice is made, they may remember their birth home as well as their birth family. Some children who were babies when they were adopted move from their birth home to the adoptive home.

Sometimes, adoption plans are made before or right at the birth of a baby. Then, the child may move from the hospital directly to the adoptive family. Sometimes the adoption plans take just a little while longer and the baby may stay in the hospital or a short term foster home until plans are finished.

If you lived in your birth home or in the hospital before your adoption, you can write about it here.

I lived in my birth home (or the hospital) this long before my adoption _____

_____

_____

Adoption plans were made for me when I was _____

_____

The people who took care of me before my adoption were _____

_____

_____

_____

Other children live in **foster homes** before adoption. These children are cared for by **foster parents.** Most of the time, the foster parents care for the child a short time until an adoptive family can be found. It is sad when some children must spend a long time in foster homes instead of being adopted quickly. Sometimes there just aren't enough foster or adoptive families for all the children who need them. Sometimes it takes a long time for birth parents, adoption and foster care workers and the courts to make decisions about how to meet a child's needs. You have already learned that adoption plans can take a long time in some cases.

Children can feel a lot of different ways about their foster parents. They can even have more than one feeling at a time. Sometimes children don't like their foster parents or feel angry about them. Sometimes children love their foster parents and other people in the family. Sometimes there are mixed feelings of love sometimes and anger other times. For some children, their foster parents are very important. For others they are not.

Foster parents may sometimes be able to make the decision to adopt a foster child who needs a family. Then, they change from people giving the child care for a short time. If they adopt a child they will always be the child's family.

If you lived in a foster home before your adoption, you can write about it here.

These are the names of my foster parents _____

_____

My foster home was in (city, state) _____

I was _____ old when I lived there.

The people in my foster home were _____

_____

If I could give a title to the story of my foster home life it would be: _____

_____

If I could describe my feelings toward my foster family in 3 words they would

be: _____ _____ _____

Other children, especially older children or children from different countries, live in **children's homes** before adoption. In some places, most children without families live in children's homes. In other places they are only used when there aren't enough foster and adoptive homes for the children who need them.

In children's homes, many different people take care of the children. These people can show a lot of love and concern for the children. There are usually many children together in a home, so there are many playmates. But sometimes it feels scary for children, especially if they miss people they care about.

If you lived in a children's home before adoption, you can write here.

My children's home was in (city, state, country) _____

I was _____ old when I lived there.

These people were special to me when I lived there _____

_____

Children waiting for adoption may live in more than one family. Some children move from place to place several times before they are adopted. Sometimes there is lots of information about where children live before adoption. Sometimes there is very little information. If you don't have much information, you can use your imagination for this.

One good thing that happened before I was adopted is _____

_____

_____

_____

One sad thing that happened before I was adopted is _____

_____

_____

_____

If I had to end my adoption story right this minute I would say that it was
(choose two)

fantastic	confusing	neverending	sad
heartwarming	secure	positive	negative
super-duper	scary	horrible	wonderful

The most important person in my life before my adoption was _____

_____

_____

This person helped me to _____

_____

_____

_____

The person who hurt me the most before my adoption was _____

_____

_____

This person hurt me by _____

_____

_____

_____

8 ARRIVAL PLANS

Before you go on, please talk about these important words with the adult helping you.

Arrival Plans are those choices that adults make about how the family will get to know one another and when they will begin to live together.

Visits are the times an adoptive family spends with their new child just before the adoption. This time is used to get comfortable with each other.

Lifebook is an album or scrapbook about a child. It may contain photos and information. A family may also have a book like this, called a family album. The two may share them during the arrival plans.

Adoptive Placement is the time when a child moves into the adoptive home.

With each adoption there are different things that happen in the days just before the family begins to live together. The **arrival plans** may depend upon many things such as the age of the child and everyone's feelings about what is happening.

Many arrival plans include **visits** between the child and the adoptive family. These visits may be at the adoption agency, the foster home, or the adoptive family's home. Visits are especially important when the child is older during the adoption process. Babies don't need as many visits before the adoption because they are so young and they don't understand what is happening.

If you had visits with your family during your adoption process, here is space for you to write about them. Ask your family to help you with the information you may need.

I had visits with my family because _____

_____

During our visits, my family felt _____

_____

During our visits, I felt _____

_____

Our visits went this way (write about how many and when you had them)

_____

_____

_____

_____

_____

During our visits, this is what we did together _____

_____

_____

_____

If I could describe our visits with a picture, this is what I remember or imagine them being like.

During the planning of the arrival, the child and the family must get ready for their new life together. The older child may talk with an adoption worker about the new family. The child may also complete a **lifebook** with an adult. This adult can help the child get ready for the **adoptive placement**. As they talk together about the move to a new family, they can fill the lifebook with photos and other things the child wants to remember. Even if the child wants to be part of an adoptive family, it can still be very scary or sad to think about changing homes. Sometimes children act mad or sad or scared about leaving. Talking about their feelings can help during this time. Completing a lifebook can be a good way to remember and to share about the child's life before the adoption. The adoptive family can begin to understand their new child by looking at the lifebook together.

If you were older when you were adopted, you can write about your arrival plans here. Ask your family to help you remember.

These are the people who helped me get ready for my adoption _____

_____

These are some of the things we did together to prepare for my adoption

_____

Here are some of the feelings I had during this time _____

_____

Here are some of the things about my new family that I was told _____

_____

If I could have changed one thing about my arrival plans it would have been

_____

The best thing about my arrival plans was _____

_____

The adoptive family always has many plans to make before the adoptive placement. If they are adopting a baby, they need to get a room and a crib ready. They may need to get other baby things like clothes and toys. They will probably want to call family and friends with the good news. Some parents are so excited they can hardly sleep at night!

If the family is adopting an older child they will need to find clothes and get the child's bedroom ready. They may also make a family album to share with the child. They can exchange the album with the child and learn about each other before the adoptive placement.

The family will have many other plans to work out. They may need to go to the adoption agency or the lawyer's office to sign papers saying they want to become a family. They may get their camera or video recorder ready so they can take pictures on the arrival day. They may call family and friends to plan for them to see their new child. They may also talk about their new child with someone who understands adoption. They may want to share both their worries and their happiness. They may have many questions about their new child. Talking with someone who knows their child can help the family get ready.

You can ask your family what they did to prepare for your arrival. Here is space for you to write about that.

My family remembers their arrival plans as being very _____

During the planning, they all felt _____ and _____

When they first found out about me they thought about _____

When they first saw my picture, they _____

These are the plans that my family had to make for my arrival _____

_____

_____

_____

_____

These are the people who helped my family prepare _____

_____

During those arrival plans, my family remembers these feelings _____

_____

Here are some special worries they had _____

_____

_____

_____

_____

Some children don't have visits with their new family because they are too young to understand about the adoption. Very young babies don't usually have visitation. In the days before this adoption it's the family, not the baby, that has many things to do. The person who is caring for the baby will get the baby ready. There may be bottles and clothes and toys to pack. There may be doctors to visit. There may be goodbye's to be said.

If you were a baby when you were adopted, here is where you can write about that. Ask your family to help you, since you will not remember those days!

During the days before my arrival, I was taken care of by _____

_____

My caretaker did these things for me _____

_____

When my family first saw me I was _____

_____

When my family first held me they felt _____

_____

_____

_____

_____

_____

_____

_____

_____

Some children do not have visits with their new parents because they must travel very long distances to get to them. These children can be babies or older children. They usually come from different countries than their new parents. Many of the arrival plans for these children have to do with transportation and getting permission for the child to come into the country. The child may talk with an adult in the birth country, too. There, the child may learn about the new family and may see a picture.

If you were adopted internationally, here is space for you to write. Ask your family to help you with the information.

These are the plans that had to be made for my trip _____

_____

_____

_____

_____

_____

These are the people who helped me prepare for my trip _____

_____

_____

When I first saw a photo of my new family, this is how I felt (use your imagination if you can't remember) _____

_____

_____

_____

_____

_____

When my family first saw me, they felt _____

_____

_____

_____

_____

_____

_____

_____

_____

_____

You may want to write a poem or story about your arrival days. If you choose to write, try to remember your thoughts and feelings, the sights and sounds of your planning time.

_____

_____

_____

_____

_____

_____

_____

_____

_____

_____

_____

_____

_____

_____

_____

_____

_____

_____

_____

_____

_____

_____

_____

_____

_____

9 THE ARRIVAL DAY

Before you go on, please talk about this important word with the adult helping you.

> **Arrival Day** is the day the child arrives to stay for good. This can also be called the adoptive placement day.

The first day joined together as a family is called the **arrival day**. This is the day the child arrives to stay for good. It's often a very special day for everyone, because everyone is so excited about becoming a family together.

If the new child is a baby, the family may be more excited than the child because they know more about what's happening. If the new child is older, the child is probably excited and nervous too. Everyone might be a little afraid. They may all feel the changes that are coming. Or, they may not stop to think about these changes. But change will happen. Things will never be the same again for anyone in the family.

No matter what feelings everyone is having, the arrival day is special. It is a new beginning for everyone in the family. The beginning might be spent with quiet, loving moments together for the first time. Or, the family may decide to go out to a restaurant to celebrate. Some families throw an adoption party. Relatives may come to visit, and people may bring gifts. Some families tell people to wait a while before they visit so the family can have time to settle. This time is important for the people to begin to feel like a family together.

Here is space for you to write about some things that happened on your arrival day. If you were very young when you were adopted, you may not remember much. Your family can help you. If you need to, you can imagine some things.

_____

_____

_____

_____

_____

_____

_____

_____

_____

_____

_____

_____

_____

_____

_____

_____

_____

_____

_____

_____

_____

_____

_____

These are the special moments I spent with my family on my arrival day

_____

_____

_____

_____

_____

The first thing that happened when I was joined with my family was _____

_____

_____

_____

_____

These were my first visitors _____

_____

_____

_____

_____

The best thing that happened on my arrival day was _____

_____

_____

_____

If my family could change one thing about that day, it would be _____

_____

_____

_____

_____

If I could change one thing about that day, it would be _____

_____

_____

_____

_____

If I had to describe my arrival day in one word, it would be _____

Arrival day is usually planned to be a happy day for everyone. But there are often so many things to do, new people to meet, and mixed up feelings that it can be a hard day. It can be confusing and tiring for everyone. It can be hard for people to enjoy the day because of these things. If people are nervous they may try to act extra nice. It may be hard for other people to be on their best behavior.

When people are nervous and worried they may act many different ways. They may be extra nice, smile a lot, be very quiet, or very loud. They may laugh, cry, or yell a lot. Some people even argue or have temper tantrums. Others run around a lot, eat a lot or too little. Others feel a little sick or very tired. Families can act these ways. Children can too.

Some people say that arrival day was like a dream come true for them. Other people remember parts of the day like a scary dream. Both feelings are normal. Families and children have different feelings and actions because people are all different.

Even if you don't remember your arrival day, your family probably does. They may remember special feelings about that day. They may remember special worries they had. They may remember exactly how everyone acted. Or, if it's been a long time since your arrival, some memories may be a little foggy. You can talk with your family about the feelings of that day, and use this next space to write about it. If you were very young or don't remember your arrival day, you may need help writing about it.

On my arrival day, my family acted like _____

_____

_____

The funniest thing that happened on my arrival day was _____

_____

_____

The good feelings my family remembers are _____

_____

_____

_____

The scary feelings my family remembers are _____

_____

_____

The nervous feelings my family remembers are _____

_____

_____

That day was a _____ day for me.

This is how I acted on my arrival day _____

_____

_____

_____

_____

This is what I wish could have happened on my arrival day _____

_____

_____

_____

The scary feelings I remember or imagine are _____

_____

_____

The good feelings I remember or imagine are _____

_____

_____

The nervous feelings I remember or imagine are _____

_____

_____

This is what I am most happy about my arrival day _____

_____

_____

_____

_____

_____

_____

Here are some of the first photos that I have of me and my family.

10 ADJUSTMENT

Before you go on, please talk about this important word with the adult helping you.

>**Adjustment** is learning to live together successfully as a family. Adjustment often takes a long time and lots of courage. It can be difficult to do.

Whenever someone new comes into a family there must be a time of **adjustment**. Parents must make adjustments when a child is born. Whole families must adjust to a new marriage. Family and child must adjust when there is an adoption. Adjusting means working hard at becoming a successful family. It means learning about the good and the bad parts of relationships. It means learning to love one another. Adjustment is often hard and slow. Sometimes, though, a family adjusts quickly when a child is adopted. Quick adjustments are nice, but not everyone has them. Adjustment can also be painful, especially when the child is older and has many memories of life before the adoption.

In a lot of ways, adjustment is something that happens throughout the time you grow up in a family. But much of the adjustment takes place right after the adoption. Adjustment, for many people, is a lifelong thing. We adjust to being a child in a family. Then, we become adults and adjust to a new family in which we are the adults.

Families find adjustment difficult for many reasons. They must change their schedule, their food, their conversation, their desires, and much more to make room for a child or to add another child to the family. Children find adjustment difficult for the same reasons. They must change their schedule, their food, their behavior, their interests and activities, even sometimes their language, their name, and their religion to accomodate new parents and a whole new family. Even babies must make adjustments when moving into new families. Sounds and touches they are used to are gone. New sights and smells are in their place. Voices and hands the baby knew are no longer there. Sometimes even food can taste different.

During adjustment people in the family may act differently at times. Some people cry often during adjustments. Other people yell a lot. Some act silly, or very noisy. Others are over active or misbehave a lot. Some people sit quietly or hide in their rooms.

Here you can write about how everyone in your family acted during your adjustment.

During our adjustment, the people in my family acted like this _____
_____
_____

During the adjustment I acted like this _____
_____
_____

These are some things I had to change during the adjustment _____
_____

These are some things my family had to change _____
_____

If I could only use two words to describe our adjustment, they would be
_____ and _____

If the adjustment period was a chapter in my life's story, it would have this title _____

Many family members are confused about these strange feelings and behaviors that can show up during adjustment. It can help to know that it's normal to have them. You and your family can work together to help each other through difficult times. The most important thing to remember about adjustment is that it's difficult for everyone— family and child— and that it takes time and effort from everyone to make the new family work.

Many people can help you with these normal parts of adjustment. Other adoptive families can be of help. You may find it helpful to talk to the parents and the children about what they went through. Perhaps they could help you understand your adjustment a little better. Adoption workers can help too. Family and friends, clergypeople, counselors and therapists are some others who could help. It is important to let people help because everyone needs others while they make important changes.

Sometimes people remember things differently from one another. Sometimes they have different opinions about the same events. You may find this to be true when you talk with your family about adjustments. There may be some things, or many things, you don't remember. You may find some things hard to understand about this time, especially if you were young when you arrived. Use your imagination if you need it, and think about the feelings you and your family had during adjustment. Ask your family to share with you so that you can complete this section.

When I had to make changes in my life I felt like _____

_____

_____

_____

My family must have looked at me and thought _____

_____

_____

Even now, adjusting to new things is _____

_____

_____

_____

When my family had to make changes, they felt _____

_____

_____

_____

I would look at my family during adjustment and think _____

_____

_____

Now, we all feel _____

_____

_____

_____

If I could change one thing about that adjustment period it would be _____

_____

_____

_____

_____

_____

If my family could change one thing it would be _____

_____

_____

_____

_____

_____

Because of the adjustment, we all learned _____

_____

_____

_____

_____

_____

_____

_____

_____

11 HELP DURING ADJUSTMENT

Before you go on, please talk about these important words with the adult helping you.

> **Counselor** is a person trained to give advice and information.

> **Therapist** is a person who can help people be healthy, and can help them to heal their hurts and to make adjustments.

During the adjustment period after an adoption, an adoption worker may visit the family. The worker may need to help the family understand one another and learn to live together successfully. Other people may also help. We all need help at times. The good thing about having people helping you during adjustment is that they can share ways that you can make your adjustment work. It can be good to know someone is watching out for you during the adjustment period.

Families with very young children may not need a lot of help. But, sometimes they do. Many families with older children may need help from a **counselor** or **therapist** right away. This can help everyone in the family from the very beginning. The counselor or therapist can help the family settle in and learn to adjust to the normal changes that take place in the family. Children or parents can talk with someone by themselves or together. They can also be part of a group that is talking about the same kinds of changes.

Counselors and therapists usually go to school to learn how to help people this way. There are other adults who can help because they have lived through adjustment and adoption and understand what it's like. Your family or your adoption worker can find a counselor or therapist if you need someone to talk to.

Here is a place to write about how you and your family were helped during adjustment.

These are the people who helped us during adjustment _____

_____

_____

These are the things we worked on with those helpers _____

_____

_____

_____

_____

_____

_____

Here are some things we learned from the people who helped us _____

_____

_____

_____

_____

_____

_____

(If you went to a counselor or therapist . . .)

My counselor or therapist helped us to _____

_____

_____

_____

_____

_____

_____

Things we are still working on that the counselor or therapist helped us with

_____

_____

_____

_____

_____

_____

(If you did not go to a counselor or therapist . . .)

This is what I think I could use some help in _____

_____

_____

_____

_____

_____

If I went to a counselor or therapist, I would _____

_____

_____

_____

_____

_____

_____

12 HOW I FEEL

Now you can think about your feelings. How did you feel during adjustment? Are you still going through adjustment? What were the things you remember the most about it? Who were the people who helped you the most? These are all memories and feelings you can use in this part.

Think of a poem or short story, or a picture that would show what your adjustment was like. If you don't remember your adjustment, that's okay. You can decide what to do based on the information you got from your family. Don't forget to use your imagination!

13 FINALIZING THE ADOPTION

Before you go on, please talk about these important words with the adult helping you.

Finalization is the process of making an adoption legal. It is the law that all adoptions must be finalized. It involves a lot of paperwork and meeting a judge who will sign the legal papers that say the adoption is for always.

Court is the place where judges work making decisions about the law. Adoptions are finalized in court.

After a child is in an adoptive home for a while, the child's family must obey the adoption laws with **finalization**. A lawyer will help the family with the papers that are sent to the court. A judge looks at these to make sure all the adoption laws are followed. The judge also looks to see that the adoption is working. When the judge makes the decision that the adoption should be forever, papers must be signed. One of the papers says that the child and the family are legally and forever a family.

Sometimes finalization does not feel as important to families as the day their child joined the family. This is because by the time they finalize, they may already feel like a family. But it is very important. It makes the adoption official. It makes it final. It says to the world that the family loves each other and wants to be a family together forever.

You may or may not remember your finalization day. You can ask your family to share with you about it. Here is a place for you to write about it.

The day I went to court to finalize my adoption was _____

The name of the judge was _____

The courthouse was located in (city and state) _____

For my family, finalization felt like _____

_____

_____

_____

_____

For me, finalization felt like _____

_____

_____

My family says finalization was _____

_____

_____

Here is a place for pictures of you and your family on finalization day.

14 NATURALIZATION

Before you go on, please talk about these important words with the adult helping you.

Citizen is a member of a country because of being born there or choosing to become a member of that new country.

Naturalization is the process of becoming a citizen of a new country.

Rights and Responsibilities of Citizenship are the privileges of belonging to a country (rights) and the way a person must act by belonging to that country (responsibilities).

Children who were not born in the same country as their adoptive families must become **citizens** of their new country. Becoming a citizen of your new country is called **naturalization**. Since your parents are already citizens of this country, you have the automatic right to become a citizen. To become a naturalized citizen a child must wait a while after the adoption is finalized. Then, the family applies for citizenship for the child. When the big day arrives, the child and the family go to the court where a judge declares the child a citizen. This is a special day. With this new citizenship, the child gains all the **rights and responsibilities of a citizen**.

You can talk with your family about those rights and responsibilities next. If you were naturalized, you can write here. You can ask an adult to help you.

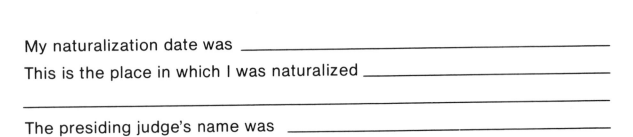

My naturalization date was _____

This is the place in which I was naturalized _____

_____

The presiding judge's name was _____

This is how I feel about being a citizen _____

_____

_____

_____

_____

Every family has opinions about what citizenship rights are. My family believes
this about rights _____

_____

_____

_____

_____

_____

_____

_____

_____

Families have opinions about citizenship responsibilities. My family believes
that the responsibilities of citizens are these _____

_____

_____

_____

_____

_____

_____

_____

This is how I feel about being a citizen of my new country _____

_____

_____

_____

_____

_____

Here, you can include a picture of you on the day you were naturalized. If you have a photo, put it here. If you don't have a photo, perhaps you would like to draw a picture. If you'd rather write about your naturalization day, then choose something about that day (a feeling, something that happened) and write a poem, a song, or a short story about it.

MY ADOPTIVE FAMILY

A very important part of your life's story is your adoptive family. The members of your family are some of the characters in your story. These are the people you live with each day. You have a special relationship with them. You are growing together, adjusting, learning to live together successfully.

You share many things in your family. You share time with one another. You share preferences, or things you like and dislike. You share values, which are beliefs. You share a religion together. These shared things are some parts of family life.

Being in a family can be an important part of being a person. Family can help us to grow up healthy. Family can help us to be happy and feel loved. We can learn to love by being in a family. When we need help or a safe feeling, family can give that.

Being in a family is also hard work. It takes hard work to live together successfully. Sometimes it takes help from other people. It takes hard work to be kind to family members. Sometimes it can be hard work to like family members. People don't always act or look the way we want them to. This makes the job of living together a difficult one at times.

This hard work of being a family happens in all families. Some families find it harder than others, but every family has these times. The thing that makes families stick together at these times is something called commitment. You can read about that in this section.

Something else that happens in all families is something called blending. Family blending happens when family members change each others lives forever. Has your family blended because of you? You can read about family blending in this section of your book.

Families are important. Families are hard work. Families take commitment. Families blend. These are all part of being a family. These are part of your life's story.

FAMILY COMMITMENT

Before you go on, please talk about this important word with the adult helping you.

> **Family Commitment** is the choice that families make to stay together. This keeps the family together when times are good and when times are hard. Commitment says the family will always be a family even if there are times when they wish they could be alone.

Have you ever wondered why a family sticks together? Do you ever argue with your family and then wonder if they still love you? Do you ever feel less love for your family? These are all normal feelings. The thing that keeps families together, even when they argue or feel less love, is **commitment.**

Commitment is a choice we make to be together. It says that even when we have bad feelings toward our family, we have decided to stay together because it's the right thing for us to do. Sometimes, it takes families a long time to make that decision. It's a very difficult decision to make. Some families may need help to make it. Other families make the choice right away. But all families share one thing. Family commitment is hard work.

Commitment can seem easy when everyone is feeling good and getting along. But when family life becomes hard, when families argue or feel hurt, commitment can be hard. Sometimes you may feel that maybe you want out of your family. Or, you may decide to change your mind about the commitment. But, keeping a family commitment pulls us through the hard times and when things get better we can again feel glad we are part of the family. Learning to keep family commitments can make us stronger adults, too. There are many job, family, and other commitments that adults must keep. People can learn how to keep these when they are young.

People who were adopted very young may not be able to make family commitment until they are older. With young children, the family makes the first commitment. That commitment says, "We will love and take care of this child and we will always be a family." This means that the family will keep that commitment through the good and hard times with the child. Later, the child will have to make the same choice. The child will have to say, "I love my family and want to stay a part of them always."

If the family or the child cannot make this commitment, the family can have trouble living together successfully. Sometimes this happens. Then, it can be good to ask for help from an adult who understands adoption, or a counselor or therapist. You may remember, these people understand the hurts that people get, and can help families heal their hurts.

People who were adopted as older children have the same commitment choices the family has. The child and the family have to decide that they will be a family through the good and the bad. This commitment decision can take a while with the older child who remembers other homes and maybe other families. It may be hard for the child to understand all about the commitment. Or, the child may have made other commitments that didn't work out. The adoptive family, too, may have worries. It can be helpful to get another person to help the family make these commitment choices.

Sometimes families cannot keep their commitments to one another even though they have tried very hard. When this happens, in some ways the family may grow apart. Sometimes this growing apart means the parents get a divorce. Or, it could mean that older children move out of the home. Sometimes adoptive families cannot keep their commitments to a child who was adopted and the family is separated from that child. Sometimes it is the child who cannot keep the family commitment. When any of these things happen, it is a very sad time. Everyone feels a lot of hurt. It can take a long, long time to heal these hurts. It may take a lot of help from counselors and therapists to heal.

Commitment can be scary. It can take lots of courage. It can sometimes make you afraid so that you want to run and hide. But keeping family commitments can make you strong. It can make you happy to know that you have people who are committed to you even when you aren't at your best. It can be a good feeling to know that you are committed to your family, even when they are not at their best.

Here, you can write about your family commitment. You can also ask your family to write about their commitment. Then, you can share your messages. Talk about them. You can find out what your family's commitment means to everyone.

MY FEELINGS ABOUT FAMILY COMMITMENT

When I think about always being part of my family I feel _____

_____

When I argue with my family I worry that _____

_____

_____

_____

_____

_____

To me, family commitment means _____

_____

_____

_____

_____

_____

These are the things that make me choose commitment to my family _____

_____

_____

_____

_____

For me, commitment was _____

_____

_____

_____

If I had to make the commitment choice again, I would choose _____

_____

_____

If I described family commitment in a picture, it would have these three colors.
_____ and _____ and _____

If I wrote a poem about family commitment, it would be mostly (choose one)

      happy   sad   sorry   crying

      smiling   soft   loud   confused

These are the things that make me happy to have family commitment

_____

_____

_____

Family commitment is sometimes hard because _____

_____

_____

_____

If I could talk with someone about this I would tell them _____

_____

_____

_____

These are the times when I most feel like making a commitment _____

_____

_____

These are the times when I least feel like making a commitment _____

_____

_____

It would help me to make a family commitment if I could _____

_____

_____

_____

(If you have had a family commitment that didn't work out . . .)

When my commitment didn't work I felt _____

_____

_____

_____

_____

It didn't work because _____

_____

_____

_____

_____

The worst thing about it was _____

_____

_____

_____

Something good that came from it was _____

_____

_____

_____

_____

If that ever happens to me again I _____

_____

_____

_____

When I think about it I worry _____

_____

_____

When I think about it I wonder _____

_____

_____

_____

MY FAMILY'S FEELINGS ABOUT FAMILY COMMITMENT

(Name of person writing: _____)

The decision to make a commitment to our child was _____

_____

_____

_____

_____

When we made the commitment we felt _____

_____

_____

_____

_____

_____

_____

_____

During the times when commitment is hard we _____

_____

_____

_____

_____

_____

_____

_____

The things that make commitment feel good are _____

_____

_____

_____

_____

_____

_____

_____

_____

2 RELATIONSHIPS

Before you go on, please talk about this important word with the adult helping you.

> **Relationship** is the connection between people. It is how people are related (sister/brother, parent/child, friend/enemy). It is why they are related (by love, by law, by blood, by adoption). Connections between people are usually a mixture of good and bad, happy and sad.

When a child joins a family something happens to that family. A new person in the family means that things will never be the same again. There is a new brother or sister. There is a new son or daughter. There is a new nephew or niece. There is a new grandson or granddaughter.

Relationships in the family change because of this new member. Everyone has a chance to know the new member. They can grow to like and even love the new member. The new family member can grow to like and love other family members. Growing together from liking to loving can be hard work. But the hard work can pay off in the end.

Sometimes people think that as more people are added to a family, there is less love to go around. But there is really enough love for everyone. Love isn't like food that gets eaten up. It's not like a clock ticking away as the hours pass by. More people in the family means more sharing, more growing, more loving. This is what being a family is all about.

When you joined your family you added some important things to everyone's life. Your family added things to your life. Here you can think about what you gave each other when you became a family. You can write about what you like about your relationship. You can write about what you don't like. This can help you to better understand your family and where you fit into it.

This is what my family says I added to the family: _____

_____

_____

_____

_____

This is what I think I added to the family _____

_____

_____

_____

_____

These are the things that changed in my family when I arrived _____

_____

_____

_____

_____

This is what my family added to my life _____

_____

_____

_____

_____

These are the things that changed in my life when I became part of my family

_____

_____

_____

_____

Some parts of our relationship that I don't like are _____

_____

_____

_____

_____

Some parts of our relationship that my family doesn't like are _____

_____

_____

_____

_____

_____

Some of the nicest things about being part of my family are _____

_____

_____

_____

_____

_____

Some of the things my family likes most about our relationship are _____

_____

_____

_____

_____

Two things I'd like to change about my relationship with my family are _____

_____

_____

_____

_____

Two things my family would like to change in our relationship are _____

_____

_____

_____

_____

The things that make me feel good about my family are _____

_____

_____

_____

_____

_____

_____

3 FAMILY BLENDING

Before you go on, please talk about this important word with the adult helping you.

> **Family Blending** is the growing together that a family does. This blending changes them from separate people with separate lives to people who share living, growing, and working. Blending makes separate people into families.

Although you don't stop being your own person, living in a family means being part of a group. The family is a very important group of people. To live together successfully, family members must blend. They must learn to share many things. Things shared may be money, food, feelings, clothes, beds, books, and many other things. Family members must learn to make choices that are good for the whole family and not just themselves. Some choices that must be made are where to live, what jobs to hold, what to buy.

Sharing of things and choices can be hard at times. People don't always agree on these things. This is part of the hard work of the family. This is where commitment is important. When we disagree, we can know that our family commitment will get us through.

Family blending is a lot like blending colors. Let's try a blending experiment. If you painted a picture of yourself, what color would you be: blue or red? (Choose only one.) If you painted a picture of your family before you joined, what color would it be: blue or red? (Choose the other one.) Use these two colors to draw a picture of your family on the next page. (You could draw a heart if you don't want to draw your family.) Crayons will work best. Use one crayon first and draw the picture. Color it in the way you want it. It works best if you press hard and make the color dark. Then, with the other crayon, color over the picture, pressing hard again.

The two colors together make a new color. You blended the colors. The two colors together make purple. Families are like this picture. There are separate colors in this picture. Blended together they form a new color. There are separate people in a family. Blended together, they become one new family.

Before you go on, please talk about this important word with the adult helping you.

> **Word Hugs** are kind and loving words that feel as good as a hug. Some word hugs are: I love you, I'm glad you are my child, You are so special to me.

One of the nice things about belonging to a family is that you can share good times and bad times. You can share all kinds of feelings. Talking and sharing in a family helps you enjoy the good things more. It can also help to make the hard things easier.

Sometimes it's hard to put feelings into words. Or, life may get so busy that families forget they need to share. But everyone needs to know how his family feels about him.

Families can share their love in many ways. But it's really important to hear about it. Hearing about those loving feelings can make people very happy.

There are many messages you can give to people. Hugs with your body may say, "I love you," or "I'm happy right now." Hearing loving words feels like someone hugged you inside. These could be called **word hugs**. Everyone needs a lot of both kinds of hugs every day.

Sometimes we need hugs or word hugs and we don't know how to ask for them. Sometimes we don't know that we need them and we just act funny because we don't feel right. There are many ways to ask for them. You can say, "Please give me a hug," or "I need to sit with you a while," or "Do you love me?" If you give some hugs, often the other person will hug back. When you give someone a hug, don't they usually hug back? Try saying, "I love you" to your family. See what happens!

Word hugs can be one of those things that needs blending in a family. People have different word hugs that they use. As new people join a family, the family can change its word hugs to meet everyone's needs.

Next, you and your family can share some special messages with each other. First, you can write down some of your feelings. Then, you can ask people in your family to write their special messages to you. Then, you can share these messages by reading them to each other, or by reading them quietly to yourself. Some people you might ask to write messages to you are: parents, brothers or sisters, aunts or uncles, grandparents.

MY SPECIAL MESSAGES TO MY FAMILY

When I joined the family, we had to blend our hugs in this way _____

_____

_____

_____

_____

This is what I do when I need to hear special messages from my family _____

_____

_____

_____

_____

These are the word hugs I like to hear most _____

_____

_____

_____

_____

When I hear those hugs I feel _____

_____

_____

_____

_____

I feel most loved when I hear _____

_____

_____

_____

_____

This is what people can tell me that makes me feel important _____

_____

_____

_____

_____

These are some people who give me word hugs _____

_____

_____

_____

_____

This is the time when I most need an arm hug _____

_____

_____

_____

_____

When I feel sad, this is the message I most need to hear _____

_____

_____

_____

_____

When I feel proud of myself, this is the message I most need to hear _____

_____

_____

_____

_____

The two people who give the best word hugs are _____

_____ and _____

They do it best because _____

_____

_____

_____

_____

_____

SPECIAL MESSAGES FROM MY FAMILY

(Name of person writing: _____)

I am special to you because _____

_____

_____

_____

_____

This is what I do best to show you I care _____

_____

_____

_____

_____

Your favorite word hugs from me are _____

_____

_____

_____

_____

The three things you like best about me are _____

_____

_____

_____

_____

When you need hugs or word hugs from me, this is what you do _____

_____

_____

_____

_____

These are the word hugs you need to hear from me _____

_____

_____

_____

_____

SPECIAL MESSAGES FROM MY FAMILY

(Name of person writing: _____)

I am special to you because _____

_____

_____

_____

_____

This is what I do best to show you I care _____

_____

_____

_____

_____

Your favorite word hugs from me are _____

_____

_____

_____

_____

The three things you like best about me are _____

_____

_____

_____

_____

When you need hugs or word hugs from me, this is what you do _____

_____

_____

_____

_____

These are the word hugs you need to hear from me _____

_____

_____

_____

_____

SPECIAL MESSAGES FROM MY FAMILY

(Name of person writing: _____)

I am special to you because _____

_____

_____

_____

_____

This is what I do best to show you I care _____

_____

_____

_____

_____

Your favorite word hugs from me are _____

_____

_____

_____

_____

The three things you like best about me are _____

_____

_____

_____

_____

When you need hugs or word hugs from me, this is what you do _____

_____

_____

_____

_____

These are the word hugs you need to hear from me _____

_____

_____

_____

_____

SPECIAL MESSAGES FROM MY FAMILY

(Name of person writing: _____)

I am special to you because _____

_____

_____

_____

_____

This is what I do best to show you I care _____

_____

_____

_____

_____

Your favorite word hugs from me are _____

_____

_____

_____

_____

The three things you like best about me are _____

_____

_____

_____

_____

When you need hugs or word hugs from me, this is what you do _____

_____

_____

_____

_____

These are the word hugs you need to hear from me _____

_____

_____

_____

_____

SPECIAL MESSAGES FROM MY FAMILY

(Name of person writing: _____)

I am special to you because _____

_____

_____

_____

_____

This is what I do best to show you I care _____

_____

_____

_____

_____

Your favorite word hugs from me are _____

_____

_____

_____

_____

The three things you like best about me are _____

_____

_____

_____

_____

When you need hugs or word hugs from me, this is what you do _____

_____

_____

_____

_____

These are the word hugs you need to hear from me _____

_____

_____

_____

_____

SPECIAL MESSAGES FROM MY FAMILY

(Name of person writing: _____)

I am special to you because _____

_____

_____

_____

_____

This is what I do best to show you I care _____

_____

_____

_____

_____

Your favorite word hugs from me are _____

_____

_____

_____

_____

The three things you like best about me are _____

_____

_____

_____

_____

When you need hugs or word hugs from me, this is what you do _____

_____

_____

_____

_____

These are the word hugs you need to hear from me _____

_____

_____

_____

_____

SPECIAL MESSAGES FROM MY FAMILY

(Name of person writing: _____)

I am special to you because _____

_____

_____

_____

_____

This is what I do best to show you I care _____

_____

_____

_____

_____

Your favorite word hugs from me are _____

_____

_____

_____

_____

The three things you like best about me are _____

_____

_____

_____

_____

When you need hugs or word hugs from me, this is what you do _____

_____

_____

_____

_____

These are the word hugs you need to hear from me _____

_____

_____

_____

_____

5 FAMILY TRADITIONS

Before you go on, please talk about this important word with the adult helping you.

> **Family Traditions** are unique ways a family celebrates holidays and special occasions. Part of these traditions is choosing everyday things that will become special occasions.

Every family has unique ways to celebrate holidays and other special occasions. These unique ways are called **family traditions**. Family traditions also may need to be blended. When new people join the family, they may be used to different traditions. The new family can blend everyone's separate traditions into brand new ones.

One of the nicest things about family traditions is that everyone can share them together. There are times when the whole family may decide to be together. There are times when you may do special things, or eat special foods. You may give gifts. You may go on trips to visit people or places. There are many ways to celebrate traditions.

Family traditions can be holidays your family celebrates during the year. These can be different for each family. Birthdays are other traditions. Traditions also include those everyday things your family decides to celebrate. Some everyday celebrations might have to do with the first day of school, or losing a tooth for young children. For older children they may be special treats after a ball game, or time alone with mom or dad.

Family traditions are an important part of being in a family. They can remind you of the good things about family: the love, the sharing, the happiness. Talk with your family about your traditions. Then, you can write about them.

Our favorite holiday is _____

This is the reason it's our favorite _____

_____

_____

_____

For that holiday, we do these special things _____

_____

_____

_____

_____

_____

Here are some other traditions in my family. Remember those everyday things that your family makes tradition.

Tradition	Special Foods	Special Activities

6 FAMILY VALUES

Before you go on, please talk about this important word with the adult helping you.

Family Values are the beliefs that a family shares about the way they should act, the way they should believe, the way they should think, and what's important to them.

Values are beliefs people have about many different things. There are values about what is right and wrong. There are values about what is important in life. There are values about what people should believe and think. Values have to do with things like work, citizenship, personal faith, money, belongings, responsibility, school. In a family, shared values are called **family values**.

Families usually share values because over the years the adults teach the children the values they want them to have. Children don't always know all of their family's values. It takes a long time to understand about values. Even adults can't always tell exactly what all their values are.

Values are different from family to family. Some families have almost the same values as others. Some families have very different values from others. Sharing the same values is one thing that makes a family feel close together. Whatever the values, doing the things that your family believes in can be a good way for family members to feel close. It can be a way to understand each other better. Sharing the important things in life are part of being a family

Family values, too, must blend. When people join the family, everyone may have to change some values. This is another way families learn to live together successfully. Often, the adults have very set values. The children may be just forming their values, or may have some set values, too. There can be hard work with blending values. Values are sometimes hard for people to change. This is part of the adjustment in becoming a successful family.

Sometimes you have to think hard about what your values really are. It can be hard to put them into words. You may want to look at this writing section with your family to help you think. Then, you can talk with your family and write about your answers.

My family says that the three most important things to remember in life are

_____

_____

_____

It is important to my family to spend a lot of time doing these things _____

_____

_____

_____

In my family, the most important goals to work for are _____

_____

_____

_____

This is what my family believes about work _____

_____

_____

_____

If we could write a story about what our family believes about treating other people, the most important things in the story would be _____

_____

_____

_____

This is what school means to my family _____

_____

_____

_____

In my family, good citizenship means _____

_____

_____

_____

In my family, the most important belief to hold is _____

_____

_____

_____

We talked about our values about school, work, money, God, life, family, citizenship, and other things. Here is a list of these values in order. Our most important values are first. The other values follow. The values that are least important are last.

_____

_____

_____

_____

_____

_____

7 FAMILY RELIGION

Before you go on, please talk about these important words with the adult helping you.

Religion is a set of beliefs and practices about God. There are many different religions with many different beliefs and practices. Many people practice a religion, but some do not.

Place of Worship is a place where people of the same religion come together to show their love for God.

Many families, as part of their values, practice a **religion**. There are many different religions and many different **places of worship**. Sharing religion together can make a family feel close and stronger. This is especially true if religion is important to the family members. It can give family members a common goal and purpose. Perhaps your family worships at a church, a synagogue, a mosque, or some other place. Wherever you worship, whichever religion you practice, you share something very special.

When a new person joins a family, a religion is something that may need to be blended. The new family member may have different religious beliefs than the rest of the family. Everyone in the family needs to talk about what to do when this happens. Religion is something that can be very personal and very strong. It can be hard to blend religious beliefs.

Some families with different religious beliefs practice separate religions. This can work if everyone in the family respects one another's beliefs. Family members can share with each other about their own beliefs. Different beliefs don't have to be a serious problem. It may take a little extra effort to make things work out.

You can talk to your family about your religion and how you practice it. Then you can write about it here.

My family worships at _____ (name your place of worship)

We practice this religion _____

These are some things we do at our place of worship _____

_____

_____

_____

_____

_____

_____

_____

_____

These are our most important religious beliefs _____

_____

_____

_____

_____

_____

_____

_____

_____

_____

_____

These are the ways we blended our religious beliefs when I joined the family

_____

_____

_____

_____

_____

_____

_____

_____

_____

(If you practice different religions in your family . . .)

This is how we work out having different beliefs in our family _____

_____ _____

_____

_____

_____

_____

_____

_____

_____

_____

_____

_____

_____

8 FAMILY PREFERENCES

Before you go on, please talk about this important word with the adult helping you.

> **Family Preferences** are the likes and dislikes family members share because they live and work together. Many of these likes and dislikes blend over time. They may include: food, clothing styles, the way they talk, things they do, hobbies they share, the way they act, family rules, word hugs they use. There are always some preferences that family members do not share because they are still separate people. This is okay.

Just as everyone inherits traits from his birth parents, everyone learns preferences from his family. These learned preferences come from the family that we grow in. They are **family preferences**. As families grow together, they begin to share preferences.

A new child adds many things to the family. The child might add a beautiful smile or a happy laugh. The child might add loud crying or soft whimpering. The child will add things the family is happy and sad about. This is what happens when any family changes because of a new person. It happens when a child is born to a family as well as when a family adopts a child.

The family, too, has some things that the child must grow to accept. The child may have different tastes in foods. The family and child may learn to change food tastes together. The child may have different religious beliefs. The family may have to learn about the child's religious beliefs to understand their child. The child may be of a different race than the family. The family may need to learn to enjoy traditions from the child's culture. There are many things that the family may need to change to learn to live together successfully. These changes begin during adjustment. Eventually child and family may grow and change enough so that they share likes and dislikes.

In all relationships there are things people like and things they don't like. For example, in parent and child relationships, parents might like to see their children get along with other people; children might like to have their parents read to them. Parents might not like their children to disobey; children might not like their parents to yell.

All relationships have the good and the bad. This is part of life. This is part of being human. There are many likes and dislikes among family members that may not be shared. This is because people still have their own ideas. People don't always agree on everything.

When children are adopted (especially older children), there are usually many preferences that the family does not share with the child. These different preferences often change with time. There are always at least a few likes and dislikes that the family members don't share, though. It's important to remember that this is okay.

It's often nobody's fault that all preferences aren't shared. It's just part of having relationships. Our preferences often can and should be changed. Often, though, they are things that can't be changed. It's good to know what we like and don't like. Sometimes that helps us understand why we act a certain way.

Preferences can be about food, clothes, things to do, TV shows, books, movies, friends, how we talk, what we talk about, and many other things. If you were a baby when you were adopted, you may have disliked your family's food or schedule. If you were older, there may have been even more differences between your preferences.

One thing about being a family is that we often start out with different preferences, but we learn to grow and change with time. This happens so the family can live together successfully. Shared preferences can make family members closer. It gives you something to do together. It can make you feel a special part of your family. You can talk with your family about the preferences you share. Then, you can write about them here.

These are the changes in preferences my family made when I joined the family

_____

_____

These are the changes in preferences that I made when I joined the family

_____

_____

_____

Our favorite foods are _____

_____

Important family rules are _____

_____

_____

_____

_____

In my family, when you're angry it's okay to _____

_____

_____

_____

Here are some ways my family shows other feelings _____

_____

_____

_____

This is one of our favorite word hugs _____

_____

These are our favorite things to do together _____

_____

_____

_____

_____

Here are some preferences that I don't share with my family _____

_____

_____

_____

_____

9 FAMILY TIME TOGETHER

Before you go on, please talk about this important word with the adult helping you.

> **Family Time** is the time that a family spends together. It is a time that can be planned or can just happen. It can be a very special sharing time for the family. Some families spend it doing special things together. Others just enjoy being with each other. It's a good time to share hobbies or to talk about ideas.

One thing that families can do together that makes them feel close and special to one another is to spend time together. This is sometimes called **family time**. Often, the family doesn't even talk about this time as 'family time.' Yet, those special times together are indeed family time.

There are many ways to share family time. Some families enjoy sports or games for family time. Other families enjoy music or reading or TV watching. Some families make a time to talk with each other about what has been happening, what they think or feel, and any problems they may have. Some families have a special time each day or week that they always spend with each other. Maybe they do the same thing each time. Family time is a chance to spend time just with each other, as a family.

Your family's time together is important because it gives you a chance to know one another better. It can help you feel the love and support only a family can give. Think hard about the times your family spends together. Talk with your family about those times. Then you can write about them here.

If I could choose something to do during family time it would be _____

_____

_____

_____

_____

113

When we spend time together, we usually do this _____

_____

_____

_____

_____

_____

If I could change one thing about our time together it would be _____

_____

_____

_____

_____

_____

_____

_____

The best time my family ever spent together was _____

_____

_____

_____

_____

_____

_____

_____

It was the best because _____

_____

_____

_____

_____

_____

_____

_____

The worst time we spent together was _____

_____

_____

_____

_____

_____

It was the worst because _____

_____

_____

_____

_____

_____

_____

The time together that makes us feel the closest is _____

_____

_____

_____

_____

_____

_____

The family time that I would like more of is _____

_____

_____

_____

_____

_____

If I could describe our family times in one word, that word would be _____

_____

Here is a page for you to put pictures of your family during family time. You could use photos, or you could draw the pictures. With each picture, you can put the names of the people and what they are doing. This will help you to remember these times.

10 FAMILY TREE

Here is a family tree. When it is all filled in, you will be able to look at it and see all the people in your family that are related to you. Sometimes it's hard to find all the dates for a family tree. The names are usually easier to find. Some of the older people in your family may be able to help you with the names and dates. You could ask your parents, grandparents, and aunts and uncles to help you. One of the nicest things about doing a family tree is the sharing you can do with family members.

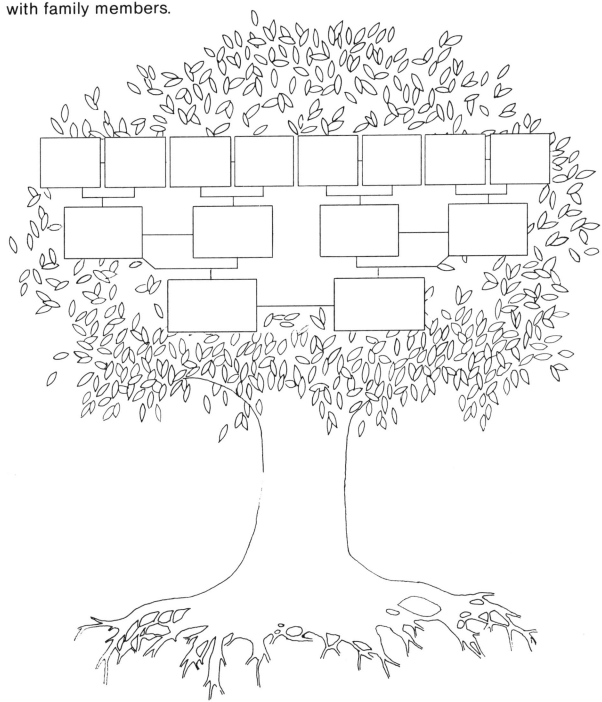

11 FAMILY PICTURES

Here are some pages for you to put pictures of your family. You can use photos and drawings. With each picture, put the names of the people and what they are doing. You may also want to put the date of the picture. This will help you to remember when you are older and look at your book.

MY SELF

Every story has a main character. You are the main character in your life's story. The whole story is really about you. It's about why adoption plans were made for you. It's about how you feel about being a person who was adopted. It's about the families that you are a part of and what they mean to you. It's about your choices and your ideas. It's about your interests and your wishes. It's about who you have been, who you are and who you are becoming.

What does it mean to be you? How would a friend describe you to a stranger? What are the words that describe you? What feelings do you have the most? How do you treat other people? What important questions do you ask yourself? What do you imagine you will be doing in 10 years? Who are the people who have been important to you? Why are they important? What does it mean to be an individual? What are your favorite things to do when you're by yourself? Who are the people who make you feel safe? How are you growing and changing? What choices do you have in life?

These are all things that you can think about as you do this part of your book. Here, you can look at yourself. You can think about how you see yourself. You can look at how you are growing and changing. You can read about yourself as an individual. You can find out about some choices that you can make with your life.

Everyone is part of a family. Sometimes that family is far away. Sometimes it's an uncomfortable relationship. Sometimes the family is a strong, stable one. People who were adopted are part of more than one family. But even family members are individuals, too. We all have times when we are alone, either because we want to be or because we have to be alone.

If we really think about it, we can see ourselves as people separate from others as well as a part of others. Understanding and liking that separate person is an important part of growing up. It can take a long time to like yourself as an individual. Thinking about yourself as an individual can help you to grow and change and to become the person you want to be.

This part of your book can help you look at yourself. It can help you think about you as a person. What kind of person are you? When you look at yourself separate from your family, what do you see? Here, you can find out. Here, you can think about how you feel about YOU! You can learn about what it really means to be the author of your own story.

1 AN INDIVIDUAL

Before you go on, please talk about these important words with the adult helping you.

Individual is one person. Everyone is an individual. Even members of large groups are individuals. Individuals are as different from each other as families can be different. They are as different from each other as adoption stories can be different.

Unique means that a person is different from everyone else in the world. Even though people share some traits, no two people in the world are exactly alike.

Personality is the way a person thinks and acts that makes that person unique. Although everyone has many different thoughts and actions, people usually act mostly one way. There are many things that make up a person's personality. Some things can be the way we talk, the way we act around family and friends and the feelings that we share. Personalities can change. People can decide to change their personalities if they want to.

You are part of two families. You have a birth family and an adoptive family. These families may be large or small. Yet, you are also an **individual**. There are things about you that make you like no one else in the whole world. You are **unique**!

Your unique qualities make you special. They make you like no one else, even though you are also like other people. You have many of the same needs that others have. You need clothing, food, water, shelter, love. Yet, you need some things that no one else may need. Perhaps you need certain word hugs that others find less important. Perhaps you need to share some ideas that your friends don't share. Maybe you need to be alone when others in your family need to be together. There are many other needs that make individuals unique.

Your interests may be unique, too. Do you share all your family's interests, or do you have some that are yours alone? Do all your friends share your interests or is there at least one thing that makes you your own person? Do you ever feel very different from other people because of your interests? Many people your age do.

Your looks also make you unique. Even though you share family traits, no one else looks exactly like you. Even identical twins can look different to people who know them well. Your hair, your face, your skin, your shape and size are all your very own.

Some people who were adopted feel they have very unique looks. They may feel this way because they don't look at all like their adoptive parents. Sometimes these people are even of a different race than their parents. When this is true, it can help to think about other people who look just like you. Your birth family looks like you. There are other people in the world who share your looks. Do you know anyone who looks a little like you? It can help to find some people that do. Your family may be able to help you do that.

Looking different than your parents doesn't have to be hard. It can be very good if everyone thinks about how wonderful it is that we can all look different, but still love each other. Being a family doesn't depend upon looks. Family is made by commitment and hard work. Some families have members from three or four different races. These families are usually built by adoption. This kind of family can be very exciting.

You have something else about you that is unique. Your **personality** is unique. The way you think and act, the way you respond to people and events, the way you are most of the time is all part of your personality. A personality can change. It may change because of good or bad things that happen to the individual. It may change because an individual decides to change.

Do you like your personality? Do you feel comfortable with it? Or would you like to change something about yourself? Would you like to be happy more often? Would you like to show more love to your family and friends? Would you like to be different in any way? You can change and grow. It takes time. It takes courage. It takes honesty. But you can do it!

Changing yourself is like being the author of your story. You think about what you want to be. You imagine it. You think of people like that. Then you work at it just as if you were writing about it. Perhaps there's an adult in your life that you trust. That person may be able to help you with this growing and changing. You could ask that friend for help.

Now you can write about yourself as an individual. You can read each item and think about it with the adult helping you.

Being an individual is _____

If I could be any other individual in the world, I would be _____

I would be that person because _____

_____

_____

The person I would least want to be like is _____

I don't want to be like that person because _____

_____

_____

Two words that describe how I feel about being an individual are:

    great   worried   scared   excited

    sad   confused   embarassed   WOW!

The individual in my family that I'm most like is _____

I'm most like that person because _____

_____

_____

The person in my family that I'm least like is _____

I'm least like that person because _____

_____

_____

The friend I'm most like is _____

I'm most like that person because _____

_____

_____

Some unique needs that I have are _____

_____

_____

When I feel those needs I do these things _____

_____

_____

Some unique interests I have are _____

_____

_____

_____

These are the things I do because I am interested in them _____

_____

_____

_____

When I want to share my interests, I share with _____

_____

_____

_____

I share with that person because _____

_____

_____

_____

My looks are unique because _____

_____

_____

_____

This is how I feel about my looks: (choose two or three)

good	comfortable	okay	YUCK!
great	so so	satisfied	worried
different	nice	uncomfortable	

The person I look the most like is _____

I look like that person because _____

_____

_____

_____

If I could change my looks, I'd want to look like _____

126

I'd want to look like that person because _____

_____

_____

_____

If I could choose one word to describe my looks, it would be _____

My personality is most like _____

It's most like that person because _____

_____

_____

_____

If I could change my personality, I'd want it to be different in this way _____

_____

_____

_____

Right now, I would describe my personality this way _____

_____

_____

_____

Friends would describe my personality this way _____

_____

_____

_____

Family would describe my personality this way _____

_____

_____

_____

When I grow up, I want my personality to be like _____

_____

_____

When I think of changing my personality, I wonder _____

_____

_____

_____

Now you can write more about your personality. Sometimes people describe others by using animals that seem to have human traits. Have you ever heard anyone described as "quiet as a mouse?" Some people are slow paced like a turtle. Others are bouncy like a rabbit or a kangaroo. Still other people could be described like a puppy— loyal and friendly to the end. Which animal would you be like? Why would you be like that animal? Use this space to write a poem about your "animal personality." Perhaps you'd rather draw a picture. That would be fine too. You could make it funny or serious. Use your imagination!

2 QUIET TIME

Before you go on, please talk about this important word with the adult helping you.

> **Quiet Time** is the time a person spends alone. This time alone can be spent doing things that the individual needs or wants to do.

Everyone needs time to be alone. Some people call this **quiet time**. At different ages, people need different amounts of quiet time. Very young children don't need much of it. They want to be with their family more than they want to be alone. Young people need a lot of quiet time. They need time to read or think or listen to music. There are many different things people like to do while alone. They use quiet time to feel like individuals instead of only group members.

Quiet time is important for other reasons. It helps people learn about their unique interests and feelings. When you are alone you can sometimes think about yourself better than when you are with lots of people. While alone, you have time to be yourself. You can be what you want to be. You can pretend if you need to. You can imagine. You can enjoy those things that are uniquely yours.

What do you do during your quiet time? Do you listen to music? Do you read? Do you just sit and think about your friends or your day? Where do you spend your quiet time? In your room? Outside in a secret place? In the basement or the car?

If you don't have time for yourself each day, you may want to think about making this time. It can be a good way to keep yourself healthy. If your house is crowded, quiet time may be hard to find. You may need to talk with your family about how and where to do it. If you let them know why you need it, they will probably help you work it out.

There are some things you can do for yourself during quiet time. You can use it to think about who you are and who you want to become. You can think about the people you admire. You can think of how you can be more like them.

You can think about how you want to grow and change to make yourself a better person.

This kind of thinking is like being the author of your own story. You can write anything you want to. An important thing to remember is that if you choose to be a healthy person in your mind and body you *can* be a healthy person. Some people need help to be healthy, but you can do it. It may take time and hard work, but with help you can do it.

Quiet time is not just for thinking. It's also for resting. It gives you a chance to rest from relationships. It gives you a chance to be yourself, do what you want, and not have to worry about what other people think. Resting is an important part of being an individual. Just as sleep helps keep you healthy and ready for the next day, quiet time rest helps keep you healthy and ready for being with other people.

Now you can think about your own quiet times. What do you like to do during them? Where do you spend them? Do you plan them or do they just happen? How do you feel after a quiet time? These are all things you can think about while you write.

These are the things I do when I am alone _____

_____

_____

_____

I do them because _____

_____

_____

_____

My favorite place to be alone is _____

_____

_____

When I am there, I feel _____

_____

_____

_____

Quiet time helps me to _____

_____

_____

_____

This is how I plan my quite time _____

_____

_____

_____

_____

This is when I most need quiet time _____

_____

_____

_____

I need it most then because _____

_____

_____

_____

_____

This is how often I need quiet time _____

_____

_____

_____

If I don't get my quiet time, I _____

_____

_____

_____

In my family, quiet time is _____

_____

_____

_____

_____

SPECIAL PEOPLE

All of us have special people in our lives. These special people are often the ones who make you feel very good about yourself. Sometimes they say things that let you know you are a good person. They may say, "You have good ideas," or "I always like to hear what you have to say," or "I like the way you dress." Sometimes they just do things that make you feel good. They may know when to hug you or may give you a wink when no one is looking. Sometimes it's even hard to tell what makes that person special. It might just be a feeling you have that you can't explain.

Special people are good to have in your life. They make you feel good about yourself and others. They can make you feel more confident. They can help you make decisions. They can be trusted friends who know your secrets. Or, maybe they are adults whom you want to grow to be like. Often, the special people in your life are family members with whom you live and grow. Family members may know you better than anyone else. They are often the ones who can help you feel good about yourself.

Can you think of the special people in your life? Who are the people who make you feel confident, happy, good? Are they adults or people your age? Are they family or friends? Are they teachers? Counselors? Classmates? You can think about these people when you do the next part of your book.

The people who make me feel good about myself are _____

_____

_____

They make me feel good by _____

_____

_____

_____

When I am with them I feel _____

_____

_____

_____

When I am not with them I _____

_____

_____

_____

The two people who say the nicest things to me are _____

_____

_____

These are the things they say that make me feel good _____

_____

_____

_____

The two people who do the nicest things for me are _____

_____

_____

These are the things they do that make me feel good _____

_____

_____

_____

Someone who has hurt me with words said this to me _____

_____

_____

_____

It hurt because _____

_____

_____

_____

When I think about saying things to make others feel good, I want to say _____

_____

_____

_____

When I think about things I could do to make others feel good, I want to _____

_____

_____

_____

4 SOCIAL GROWTH

Before you go on, please talk about these important words with the adult helping you.

Development is the growing and changing that people do. This starts when a person is born and continues through adulthood. People never really stop growing and changing. Growth and change happen even when we don't want them to. To stay healthy during development, people may need help. Doctors, teachers, counselors and therapists, family, friends, clergypeople can all help us stay healthy.

Social Growth is the growing and changing a person does to get along with other people. Healthy social skills help keep a person healthy all over.

Peer Pressure is the influence that a person's group of friends can have. This makes a person want to be like the group and do what the group does. Peer pressure can be healthy, when the group is doing healthy things. It can be unhealthy, when the group is doing unhealthy things.

Even before a person is born, **development** begins. The tiny baby within its birth mother's body grows and changes every day. After the baby is born, it will develop for many, many years until that person dies. Development happens to us all. We grow and change every day.

We grow and change for many reasons. One reason is because of other people. Our family, our friends, even people we meet only once, or whom we never meet at all, help us to grow and change. The most important thing about development is that in many ways we can decide to grow and change. We can choose the things that keep us healthy.

One part of our development is learning how to get along with other people. This is called **social growth**. Social growth changes us. Little children always want to be first. Still later, children learn to let others go first. People your age are often uncomfortable with adults and sometimes don't like them. Later, you will learn how to get along with adults. By the time you are an adult, if you are socially healthy, you will be able to get along with most people. You may not like everyone, but you will be able to get along with them.

To stay healthy all over, you must try to stay healthy in your social growth. You may want to find out from family and friends if they think you are on the right track. Or, you could ask a counselor or therapist if you see one. Often, people your age feel uncomfortable about themselves around other people. Often they wonder if they are okay, if they are likeable. This is normal. Almost everyone goes through that time in his life.

There are some questions you can ask yourself to find out if you are staying healthy in your social growth. You could ask, "Do I think about other people's feelings when I'm with them?", "Do I try to make up with my friends when we fight?", "Do I keep friends, even when we disagree?", "Do I feel sorry when I am mean to a friend?", "Do I feel sorry when I am mean to my family?", "Do I have some good times with my family?", "Do I often feel comfortable around other people?", "Do I enjoy being with other people my age?", "Do I sometimes have trouble going against my friends?"

If you answer "yes" to most of these questions, then you are probably growing healthily for someone your age. You could ask an adult who knows you if they agree with your thoughts. It can be helpful to get someone else's opinion about this.

There are many social skills that young people can develop that can help them feel more comfortable with other people. You can work on being friendly with classmates and adults. You can try to say only good things about other people. You can work on helping friends get along. Or, you can work on getting along with your own friends.

One of the most important things to understand about being your age is **peer pressure**. When young people are together, they want to feel like they belong. (Adults have this feeling, too.) Often, belonging means you want to do what the group does. This can sometimes be good, especially if your friends are healthy people doing healthy things. Then, peer pressure can be healthy. Some healthy peer pressures are wanting to make good grades, join school clubs, be a kind friend, and do your very best in all things. But sometimes, doing what the group does can be unhealthy. When this happens, you can try to find the things to say and do that will help you stay healthy even if your friends aren't doing healthy things.

Some of the things friends want to do that are unhealthy for young people may be drugs, sex and drinking. Can you think of other things? Talking with healthy young people can help you find out what they do when they need to say NO to what their group is doing. Talking with teachers, a counselor, or parents can also help. Learning how to belong to a group while being your own person is a hard thing to do. Even some adults find this hard. Many people have been able to figure it out, though. With help, perhaps you can too!

Now you can write about your social growth. This can help you understand yourself better. Thinking about your social growth can help you feel more comfortable with your growing and changing during this time in your life. When I am with other people my age I feel _____

_____

_____

_____

When I am alone, I worry that I might be _____

_____

_____

_____

_____

If I could change one thing about myself when I am with adults it would be

_____

_____

_____

I want to change that because _____

_____

_____

_____

If I could change one thing about myself when I am with my family it would be

_____

_____

_____

I want to change that because _____

_____

_____

_____

_____

My best social skill is _____

I'm good at it because _____

_____

_____

_____

When I'm with my friends, they probably see my social skills this way _____

_____

_____

_____

_____

These are the problems I have with peer pressure _____

_____

_____

_____

_____

If I could ask for help in saying NO, I would want to ask these questions _____

_____

_____

_____

_____

The biggest problem I have with peer pressure is _____

_____

_____

_____

_____

When I'm with my friends, I wish I could feel _____

_____

_____

_____

The person my age who knows how to say NO to unhealthy peer pressure is

_____

_____

_____

5 EMOTIONAL GROWTH

Before you go on, please talk about this important word with the adult helping you.

> **Emotional Growth** is the growing and changing of thoughts, feelings and ideas. Healthy emotions help keep a person healthy all over.

Another part of growing and changing is **emotional growth**. Let's think about a baby again. A baby feels sad or happy depending upon if it's hungry, wet, messy, or needing to be held. There are many more things that make you feel sad or happy, aren't there? You have many more feelings, too. This is all because you have done a lot of emotional growing since you were born.

You are older. Now, you may let your feelings get hurt by someone's harsh words. You may get angry over a test grade, or frustrated over something your family does. You feel surprise, love, fear, and many other emotions.

To stay healthy, you must also keep your emotional growth healthy. Healthy emotional growth depends upon you. What do you choose? Do you choose to be angry and sad most of the time? Or, do you choose happiness most of the time? It's okay to have mixed feelings. But being healthy depends upon how you feel most of the time.

A positive attitude most of the time is what can keep you healthy. It can make your social life healthy, too. Some people even believe it can help your body stay healthy! Choosing healthy emotional growth is a lot like writing your own story. You can think about what you want to write, and then sit down and do it. You can think about healthy emotions and then work at growing them.

Many people find that asking for help with emotional growth is a good way to stay healthy. A counselor or therapist may be able to help. Or, family members or friends can help. Often, an adult like a teacher or clergyperson can be of help. Asking for help with emotional growth can be a good sign that you want to be a healthy person.

Now you can write about your emotional growth. Think about how you feel most of the time. What one word would describe it? Think about how you react to bad news. Do you get over it quickly or sulk for days? Think about how you feel when you are disappointed. Do you feel a balance between sadness and hope or do you feel only despair? There are many emotions that you can think about. You could ask an adult to share thoughts with you.

When I have a disappointment, I feel _____

_____

_____

_____

That feeling lasts for this long _____

_____

When I have hurt feelings, I feel _____

_____

_____

_____

I get over the hurt this way _____

_____

_____

_____

When a friend hurts me I _____

_____

_____

_____

When someone in my family hurts me I _____

_____

_____

_____

When I feel happy, this is how I act _____

_____

_____

_____

_____

Most of the time, I feel _____

_____

_____

_____

During quiet time I feel _____

_____

_____

When I think about being adopted I feel _____

_____

_____

The things that can make me feel happy are _____

_____

_____

_____

When I am with my friends I feel _____

_____

_____

_____

When I am with my family I feel _____

_____

_____

_____

Two people that make me feel good about myself are _____

_____ and _____

If my emotional growth was a color, it would be _____

If I could see my face in the mirror all the time, most of the time I would look like

_____

_____

_____

_____

PHYSICAL AND INTELLECTUAL GROWTH

Before you go on, please talk about these important words with the adult helping you.

> **Physical Growth** is the growing and changing of the body from birth through adulthood. A healthy body helps to keep a person healthy all over. But if the body is not healthy, a person can still have a healthy social, emotional, and intellectual growth.
>
> **Intellectual Growth** is the growing and changing of the mind. This includes thinking abilities like reading, math, and language. It also includes being able to solve social and emotional problems. Even if a person's mind is not able to work like most people's, the person may still have healthy social, emotional, and physical growth.

Another kind of growth is **physical growth**. This involves the body. It is an easy change to see. A baby looks very different from you or from an adult.

People your age have some important growing and changing to do. Your body is at a point when it is making the change from childhood to adulthood. You can talk with your family about those changes. It's important to understand them. There are many things you can do to keep your body healthy during this time and through adulthood.

Some people do not have what most would consider to be healthy bodies. Physical health is not something you need to stay healthy socially and emotionally. You don't need it to have a healthy mind, either. It's nice to have physical health. It can make life easier. But health all over doesn't depend upon physical health.

Another kind of growing and changing people do involves their minds. It's called **intellectual growth**. This growth changes a person's mind. It makes people able to think better, read better, use numbers better, and solve problems better the older they get. You can do more of this than a young child can. Adults can do more than you can.

Intellectual growth is good. It changes us from babies who need total care to adults who can take care of ourselves. Some parts of the mind help us with social, emotional and physical growth. Yet, there are many people who have minds that do not grow and change like most people's. Still other people have accidents and their brains are injured. These people can still have healthy social and emotional growth. Often they can have healthy bodies, too. Intellectual growth isn't always necessary to stay healthy all over.

Now you can think about your own physical and intellectual growth. You can write about it here.

When I think about my changing body I feel _____

_____

_____

_____

These are the ways my body is changing _____

_____

_____

_____

_____

If I could ask any questions about my changing body, they would be _____

_____

_____

_____

_____

(If you have a physical disability . . .)

This is how I feel about my disability _____

_____

_____

_____

If I could help other people understand my disability, I would do it this way

_____

_____

_____

_____

When I think about my intellectual growth I feel _____

_____

_____

_____

_____

The things I like to learn most are _____

_____

_____

_____

I like learning these things because _____

_____

_____

_____

These are the ways I think my mind is growing and changing _____

_____

_____

_____

_____

(If you have an intellectual disability . . .)

This is how I feel about my disability _____

_____

_____

_____

If I could help other people understand my disability, I would do it this way

_____

_____

_____

_____

7 MAKING CHOICES

Most kinds of growth can take place from birth to death, helping the person to become a better individual. This is especially true of social and emotional growth. Those are two things for which you can make many choices. You can choose to be kind to others, and to treat them with respect. You can choose to get along with people. You can choose to think about positive things and be mostly happy about life.

There are some choices you can make about physical growth that can keep you healthy, too. You can choose exercise and a good diet. You can choose to get help from the doctor and other people when you need it. The same is true with intellectual growth. You can choose to keep your mind sharp and able.

Physical and intellectual growth cannot be fully controlled even when you wish they could. They also depend upon the abilities you have at birth. Some people are born with very able bodies and minds. Other people are born with less able bodies or minds or both. Yet, these people can still choose to be healthy socially and emotionally. They can also choose to use their bodies or their minds to the best of their ability. This is healthy living. Choosing to do your very best can make you a better individual.

Now you can think about your own growing, changing and choosing. You can look at your development in all areas and think about being healthy. You can ask an adult to help you with some of this. It may be difficult to figure out just how you feel about all of this. It can be hard to choose the most important things in your life.

145

Try to remember everything you have read about the four different kinds of growth: social, emotional, physical and intellectual. If you had to put them in order of importance to you, which would go first? Which one would be second? Third? Fourth? You can put them in order here and then you can write why you chose that order. You can think and share with an adult. The order you choose may be the order in which you choose to grow and change.

1 _____

Why? _____

_____

_____

_____

_____

2 _____

Why? _____

_____

_____

_____

_____

3 _____

Why? _____

_____

_____

_____

_____

4 _____

Why? _____

_____

_____

_____

_____

8 FEELING GOOD ABOUT MYSELF

Before you go on, please talk about this important word with the adult helping you.

> **Self-Esteem** is how you feel about yourself. If you feel mostly good about yourself, you probably have a positive self-esteem. If you feel mostly bad about yourself, then you may have a negative self-esteem. Liking yourself can help you grow up healthy. Some people call this self-confidence.

When you started this part of your book, you read about learning to like yourself. How do you feel about YOU? Do you think you're a good person? Do you think you are fun to be with? If you were someone else, would you like you? Are you just the way you want to be, or do you want to change some things?

These are all questions that relate to how you feel about yourself. If you feel mostly positive about yourself, then you have a positive self-esteem. You like yourself. One of the best ways to make healthy growing and changing choices is to have a positive **self-esteem**. People who feel good about themselves can make healthy choices. This is because they can make choices that are good for them.

If you feel mostly bad about yourself, then perhaps you can find some ways to work on your self-esteem. Can you find a friend who can help? Is there someone you can trust whom you could go to and say, "Please help me make some changes that will help me to like myself"? If you can find that person, then you can work together on these changes.

You can ask for help in saying good things about yourself. You can ask that friend to listen to you talking and to remind you to look at your good points. When you begin to say negative things, your friend can remind you of the positive. You can also ask your friend to help you think positive thoughts by telling you about your good points. Positive thoughts and positive words can help you feel good about yourself.

Whether or not you find someone to help you, there are other things you can do. Try to catch yourself thinking good thoughts. Try to think often about the things you do well. Try to think often about the people whom you have helped. Try often to imagine yourself strong, happy, and healthy. When you feel sad or lonely, do something that can make you feel better.

Building positive self-esteem can be hard work. Just like many things in life, it can take courage. But positive self-esteem can help you be a stronger, healthier person. It can get you through difficult times. It can make being an individual and a family member easier and more successful.

Now you can write about your self-esteem. You can read the next part and share with an adult. You can think about how you feel and what you can do to feel even better about yourself.

When I think of me as in individual, I feel mostly _____

I would say that my self-esteem is _____

These are the things that can happen to make me feel very good about myself

_____

_____

_____

_____

_____

_____

These are the things that can make me feel negative about myself _____

_____

_____

_____

_____

_____

_____

My friends would probably say that my self-esteem is _____

_____

My family would say that my self-esteem is _____

_____

When I talk about myself, it's mostly _____

_____

_____

The person that I know with the most positive self-esteem is _____

_____

That person seems very positive because _____

_____

_____

_____

The person that I know with the most negative self-esteem is _____

_____

That person seems very negative because _____

_____

_____

_____

If I could describe my self-esteem with a color, I would be _____

I chose that color because _____

_____

_____

(If you often say and think negative things about yourself . . .)

These are the negative things that I say about myself _____

_____

_____

I say these things when I _____

_____

_____

When I'm alone, this is how I think of myself _____

_____

_____

_____

_____

_____

_____

_____

_____

_____

_____

YOUR ADOPTION STORY:
THE END AND THE BEGINNING

Here you are at the end of your book. But this is not the end of your life story. There are many things that you can add to your story.

You will do a lot of growing and changing in the next few years. What will you choose to become? Will you choose to be a happy person? Will you look for laughter and smiles? Will you feel good about yourself and what you can do? These choices will help to write the rest of your story.

Now that you know all you can about your adoption story, perhaps this is only the beginning. Perhaps this is the first time you have felt you really could begin to understand your adoption story. Maybe now you can look at the adoption plans that were made for you and say, "I understand. I accept my life the way it is." Or maybe you don't have many answers. Maybe you can come to accept the unanswered questions about your birth family and adoption plans.

Perhaps, though, you cannot say this. You may be like many people, and accepting these things may be very difficult. Well, that's okay too. The important thing is that you keep working on your life. You can make the choices that will keep you healthy. You can make the choices that will keep you successful with your family and friends.

Choose to be your own writer. Write positive things into your life. Write about happiness and health. Write about a successful family life. Write about growing and changing that makes you a better person. Use the next pages to imagine yourself in the future. How will your story continue? What will your life be like? What kind of an adult will you become? You can write your future. Choose to be a writer of a story with a happy ending!!

GLOSSARY

Adjustment is learning to live together successfully as a family. Adjustment often takes a long time and lots of courage. It can be difficult to do.

Adopt is to legally join one or more parents and a child not born to them into a family.

Adoption is the choice that adults make when birth parents cannot be nurturing parents for their children. This is when adoptive parents become the nurturing parents.

Adoption Agency is the place that brings together children who need families with families who need children.

Adoption Choices are the decisions and plans that adults make for children who need adoptive parents. Or, they are the decisions that adults make to become adoptive parents.

Adoption Laws are rules made by a government about adoption. These can be different from place to place.

Adoptive Family is the family that adopts. It can be made up of one parent or two parents and one or more children who were adopted. It can have children who were born into the family also.

Adoptive Parents are mothers and fathers who choose to nurture a child they did not give birth to.

Adoption Process is the way an adoption happens to make a new family.

Adoption Study is the way an agency learns about a family that has chosen adoption. It is also the way a family can learn more about the adoption choices it must make. During the adoption study, a family may spend time with an adoption worker and other adoptive families, talking and learning about children who need families.

Adoption Worker is the adult who helps children and parents come together as a family. This adult may also work with families after a child enters the family through adoption.

Adoptive Placement is the time when a child moves into the adoptive home.

Agency Adoption is an adoption planned with the help of an adoption agency. This agency can be a public one run by a city, county, state or other government department. Or, the agency can be a private one which has permission to plan adoptions, but is not run by the government.

Arrival Day is the day the child arrives to stay for good. This can also be called the adoptive placement day.

Arrival Plans are those choices that adults make about how the family will get to know one another and when they will begin to live together.

Birth Country is the country where a person is born.

Birth Home is the home in which the birth mother and/or father live. The child may or may not have lived there before the adoption.

Birth Language is the language of the country where a person is born.

Birth Parents are the mother and father who give life to a baby. Everyone has a birth mother and father. Some people are nurtured by their birth parents. Other people are nurtured by their adoptive parents.

Birth Siblings are brothers or sisters related by birth. These brothers or sisters may share both the same father and mother, or they may share one parent. If they share one parent it could be either the same mother or the same father.

Children's Home is a place where many children live who cannot live with their birth families. Here, they are cared for by many adults. Other names for a children's home are residence, children's center, orphanage. Some children's homes have special care for children who need help with special problems they may have.

Citizen is a member of a country because of being born there or choosing to become a member of that new country.

Counselor is a person trained to give advice and information.

Court is the place where judges work making decisions about the law. Adoptions are finalized in court.

Development is the growing and changing that people do. This starts when a person is born and continues through adulthood. People never really stop growing and changing. Growth and change happens even when we don't want them to. To stay healthy during development, people may need help. Doctors, teachers, counselors and therapists, family, friends, clergypeople can all help us stay healthy.

Emotional Growth is the growing and changing of thoughts, feelings and ideas. Healthy emotions help keep a person healthy all over.

Family Blending is the growing together that a family does. This blending changes them from separate people with separate lives to people who share living, growing, and working. Blending makes separate people into families.

Family Commitment is the choice that families make to stay together. This keeps the family together when times are good and when times are hard. Commitment says the family will always be a family even if there are times when they wish they could be alone.

Family Preferences are the likes and dislikes family members share because they live and work together. Many of these likes and dislikes blend over time. They may include food, clothing styles, the way they talk, things they do, hobbies they share, the way they act, family rules, word hugs they use. There are always some preferences that family members do not share because they are still separate people. This is okay.

Family Time is the time that a family spends together. It is a time that can be planned or can just happen. It can be a very special sharing time for the family. Some families spend it doing special things together. Others just enjoy being with each other. It's a good time to share hobbies or to talk about ideas.

Family Traditions are unique ways a family celebrates holidays and special occasions. Part of these traditions is choosing everyday things that will become special occasions.

Family Values are the beliefs that a family shares about the way they should act, the way they should believe, the way they should think, and what's important to them.

Finalization is the process of making an adoption legal. It is the law that all adoptions must be finalized. It involves a lot of paperwork and meeting a judge who will sign the legal papers that say the adoption is for always.

Foster Home is a home where some children are cared for when they cannot be with their birth families. Some children live in foster homes before adoption.

Foster Parent is the person who cares for the child in a foster home.

Independent Adoption is an adoption planned without the help of an adoption agency.

Individual is one person. Everyone is an individual. Even members of large groups are individuals. Individuals are as different from each other as families can be different. They are as different from each other as adoption stories can be different.

Inherited Traits are physical or health patterns, talents, and preferences that people have even before birth. Inherited traits come from birth parents, grandparents, and other birth ancestors.

Intellectual Growth is the growing and changing of the mind. This includes thinking abilities like reading, math, and language. It also includes being able to solve social and emotional problems. Even if a person's mind is not able to work like most people's, the person may still have healthy social, emotional, and physical growth.

International Adoption is an adoption which brings together a child from one country who needs a family with a family from another country who needs a child.

Lifebook is an album or scrapbook about a child. It may contain photos and information. A family may also have a book like this, called a family album. The two may share them during the arrival plans.

Mixed Feelings are when people have more than one feeling at the same time. Sometimes these different feelings are opposite feelings and happen all at the same time. This can make a person feel confused. Sometimes different feelings come and go one at a time. Sometimes these different feelings aren't easy to put your finger on and they make a person feel sad without knowing why. Mixed feelings sometimes make it hard to want to think about whatever gives us mixed feelings.

Naturalization is the process of becoming a citizen of a new country.

Nurture means to take care of, to help to grow, to train, to teach. Children are nurtured by parents so that they can grow up healthy and happy.

Peer Pressure is the influence that a person's group of friends can have. This makes a person want to be like a group and do what the group does. Peer pressure can be healthy, when the group is doing healthy things. It can be unhealthy, when the group is doing unhealthy things.

Personality is the way a person thinks and acts that makes that person unique. Although everyone has many different thoughts and actions, people usually act mostly one way. There are many things that make up a person's personality. Some things can be the way we talk, the way we act around family and friends and the feelings that we share. Personalities can change. People can decide to change their personality if they want to.

Physical Growth is the growing and changing of the body from birth through adulthood. A healthy body helps to keep a person healthy all over. But if the body is not healthy, a person can still have a healthy social, emotional, and intellectual growth.

Place of Worship is a place where people of the same religion come together to show their love for God.

Quiet Time is the time a person spends alone. This time alone can be spent doing things that the individual needs or wants to do.

Relationship is the connection between people. It is how people are related (sister/brother, parent/child, friend/enemy). It is why they are related (by love, by law, by blood, by adoption). Connections between people are usually a mixture of good and bad, happy and sad.

Religion is a set of beliefs and practices about God. There are many different religions with many different beliefs and practices. Many people practice a religion, but some do not.

Rights and Responsibilities of Citizenship are the privileges of belonging to a country (rights) and the way a person must act by belonging to that country (responsibilities).

Self-Esteem is how you feel about yourself. If you feel mostly good about yourself, you probably have a positive self-esteem. If you feel mostly bad about yourself, then you may have a negative self-esteem. Liking yourself can help you grow up healthy. Some people call this self-confidence.

Siblings are brothers or sisters related by birth or by adoption.

Social Growth is the growing and changing a person does to get along with other people. Healthy social skills help keep a person healthy all over.

Therapist is a person who can help people be healthy, and can help them to heal their hurts and to make adjustments.

Unique means that a person is different from everyone else in the world. Even though people share some traits, no two people in the world are exactly alike.

Visits are the times an adoptive family spends with their new child just before the adoption. This time is used to get comfortable with each other.

Word Hugs are kind and loving words that feel as good as a hug. Some word hugs are: I love you, I'm glad you are my child, You are so special to me.

ABOUT THE AUTHOR

Susan Gabel, M.Ed., is a parent, an educator, and a writer. She and her husband live in Southfield, Michigan, with their four children, who were adopted. Her family is multi-ethnic, formed through both local and international adoption. Susan was raised in an adoptive family, with a brother and sister adopted as infants. The value of adoption for both adults and children has always been an important issue to her. Susan has made several television appearances and written about adoption issues, her topics including waiting children, civil rights issues in adoption, special needs adoptions, and parent-advocacy for children who were adopted. A special education teacher, she holds a B.A. in learning disabilities. Her master's degree is in reading from Wayne State University, Detroit, Michigan. Through the years, she has also been involved with parent training and child advocacy in the field of disabilities. She is currently involved in projects that enable children with disabilities to be accepted within the community. She is a Board member of Community Opportunity Center, a nonprofit agency serving adults with disabilities in Wayne County, Michigan.

LET US INTRODUCE OURSELVES . . .

Perspectives Press is a narrowly focused publishing company. The materials we produce or distribute all speak to issues related to infertility or to adoption. Our purpose is to promote understanding of these issues and to educate and sensitize those personally experiencing these life situations, professionals who work in infertility and adoption, and the public at large. Perspectives Press titles are never duplicative. We seek out and publish materials that are currently unavailable through traditional sources. Our titles include . . .

Perspectives on a Grafted Tree

An Adoptor's Advocate

Understanding: A Guide to Impaired Fertility for Family and Friends

Our Baby: A Birth and Adoption Story

The Mulberry Bird

The Miracle Seekers: An Anthology of Infertility

Real For Sure Sister

Our authors have special credentials: they are people whose personal and professional lives provide an interwoven pattern for what they write. If **you** are writing about infertility or adoption, we invite you to contact us with a query letter and stamped, self addressed envelope so that we can send you our writers guidelines and help you determine whether your materials might fit into our publishing scheme.

Perspectives Press
P. O. Box 90318
Indianapolis, Indiana 46290-0318